Women in Business

Theory, Practice and Flexible Approaches

Published by
Adonis & Abbey Publishers Ltd
P. O. Box 43418
London
SE11 4XZ
http://www.adonis-abbey.com
Email: editor@adonis-abbey.com

First Edition, January 2010

British Library Cataloguing-in-Publication Data
A catalogue record for this book is available from the British Library

ISBN: 9781906704445(HB)/ 9781906704698

Layout Artist/Technical Editor, Jan B. Mwesigwa

Women in Business

Theory, Practice and Flexible Approaches

By

Mirjana Radović Marković
and
Imani Silver Kyaruzi

Adonis & Abbey
Publishers Ltd

ACKNOWLEDGEMENT

We would like to express our gratitude to all those who gave us the possibility to complete this book. In particular, we would like to thank the Department of Economics and Entrepreneurship, University of Krujevac, Serbia. Special thanks to Mercy Sassel, Duduzile Moyo and Rahima Rwenza-Kindblom. Also thanks to Zukrah Mattembe and Helena Kemetse of the University of Birmingham, United Kingdom.

CONTENTS

Acknowledgement.. *iv*

List of Figures and Tables.. *vii*

Preface.. *ix*

Chapter 1
Introduction: An Overview of Entrepreneurship 1

Chapter 2
The Entrepreneurship Process: Generating Ideas.................... 13

Chapter 3
Planning a New Business and Feasibility Study...................... 31

Chapter 4
Starting a Business.. 53

Chapter 5
The Characteristics of Businesses that Entrepreneurs
Do from Home.. 65

Chapter 6
Setting An Office at Home... 93

Chapter 7
Appearance and Professionalism 99

Chapter 8
The Future of home Businesses 107

Chapter 9
Setting up a Business Venture: Key Decisions 111

Chapter 10
Communication.. 121

Chapter 11
Franchising 137

Chapter 12

Conclusions 147

References 149
Index 151

List of Figures

Figure 3.1: *Activity 1:* The test – How important is your set goal?.. 41

Figure 4.2: *Activity 2* – Do you have sufficient support from your family?.................................... 58

Figure 4.3: *Activity 3* – Test whether you have the affinity for starting your own business? 61

Figure 9.4: *Activity 4* – Evaluating Your Personal Goals.... 113

Figure 9.5: *Activity 5:* Test on Finances 117

Figure 9.6: *Activity 6:* Testing your Marketing knowledge 117

Figure 9.7: *Activity 7:* Testing Your General Management Skills 118

Figure 10.8: *Communication System Model* 125

Figure 10.9: *A Single Strand Chain* 132

Figure 10.10: *The Gossip Chain* 132

Figure 10.11: *The Probability Chain* 133

Figure 10.12: *The Cluster Chain* 133

List of Tables

Table 10.1: Obstacles to Effective Communication 129

Table 11:2 Advantages of buying a franchise 143

Table 11.3: Franchising contract elements 145

PREFACE

In recent years, a record number of women have been breaking out of corporate life and embracing entrepreneurial careers as an alternative to inflexible work practices and outdated systems. Although women still face "glass ceiling" and somehow fail to achieve their maximum potential, there is evidence to suggest that most countries have now realized the potential contribution women make to their nation's economic growth. The rise of female entrepreneurship has brought in a new revolution as we see women emerge as business owners in economic sectors they have not previously occupied. This calls for new ways of "re-imagining" the roles of women in economic development. There are more flexible work arrangements allowing women to balance both work and careers.

On the business side, however, businesses that women entrepreneurs run from their homes are relatively new. These are usually smaller businesses dealing with basic products and providing other online services. Against the belief of many people who assume that these are temporary settings, these businesses are very stable and are proving to have higher survival rates than 'normal' new businesses. This is affirmed by data which illustrates that the average age of businesses which owners run from their homes is around six years. This survival rate, compared to other forms of business, is significant to the local economic initiatives. Based on these facts, women entrepreneurs are forming a very important subgroup within the economy. Findings from this research are likely to benefit entrepreneurs, institutions and those who are actively involved in policy formulation.

Women in Business sets out to provide support and to act as a guide for both established and aspiring female entrepreneurs. Some checklists and practical tests were used to make the decision-making process easier for both groups of entrepreneurs. We are fully aware that self-employment and entrepreneurial activities are decisions that cannot be taken lightly. For most women, families tend to take the first priority. The book acknowledges this and presents a balanced argument. We are optimistic that this book will be able to reach and inspire women who have, or are about to take a decision to become entrepreneurs.

Mirjana Radovic-Markovic
and
Imani Silver Kyaruzi
January, 2010

Chapter 1

INTRODUCTION:
AN OVERVIEW OF ENTREPRENEURSHIP

This book documents a novel attitude towards women entrepreneurship and self-employment. Drawing on insights from various entrepreneurship theories – it seeks to provide support and practical guidance to both aspiring and established women entrepreneurs. We do not claim to provide definitive answers or solutions to all problems facing women entrepreneurs today, but our aim is to encourage more women to become business owners and to support those who are still contemplating self-employment as an alternative to their current employment, or as a part-time activity to complement their current economic activities. As a word of caution, however, it should be noted that some problems facing women in businesses are multifaceted - they are either place or cultural-specific and thus might require different approaches from the ones highlighted in this volume. We have now set the scene for this agenda and we are optimistic that this book will provide a foundation to women who would like to venture into self-employment. The book contains eleven chapters beginning with an exploration of the history of entrepreneurship, followed by a step-by-step guidance for creating successful ventures.

The historical part of this book is intended to enable readers to identify the entrepreneurship styles and forms that fit neatly within their cultural, political, technological and social environment. The practical guides are aimed to be used as checklists for those who are about to make decisions.

The History of Entrepreneurship

Entrepreneurship is now forming an economic agenda in both developed and developing economies. However, it

1

should be noted here that entrepreneurship is not a new phenomenon; the concept has been around for many years. The
term *"entrepreneur"* was introduced in the Mercantilist age by
Richard Cantillon (1680-1734). Schumpeter (1950) notes Cantillon's work, which is described as the first systematic treatise on
economics to develop the term *"entrepreneur"*. Cantillon defines an entrepreneur as:

> "...an agent who buys means of production at certain prices
> in order to combine them into a product that he is going to
> sell at prices that are uncertain at the moment which he
> commits himself to his costs" (pp 253-54).

The author has been credited for his contribution to the
field by linking entrepreneurial activities to economic growth
and allocation of resources. These ideas were later incorporated into Say's *Treatise on Political Economy* (1821). It was later
suggested that for entrepreneurs to be able to play a role in
economic activities, allocating resources and profit-making,
there is a need for capital. Those who followed, for instance,
Adam Smith, built his argument along similar concepts by
claiming that *"...an entrepreneur is best understood using capital
and risks"*. He considered a case of the capitalist who lends his
money to other people and so recognizes the special function
of people who take on the use and risk of capital. Entrepreneurs are those who take risks of the new (and existing) enter-
prises.

In a similar vein, one of the famous economists John Stewart Mill (1806-1973) also noticed that taking risks should be
part of the entrepreneurial function. However, the ideas of
economic growth and risk-taking were further challenged by
other thinkers as they sought to take the concept to another
level. The economic view has had little mention of an entrepreneur and his roles in the economic process. For example,
Say (1803), in his book titled *"Tractate of Political Economy"*, emphasized the importance of entrepreneurs. He defines an entrepreneur as:

"...a person who moves economic resources from the area of lower to the area of higher productivity and greater profit".

Based on this view, Say defines the function of an `entre-preneur` independently of a social framework and the issue of risk-taking is not included in the definition. Other authors who extended this argument, for example, Knight (1921) provided a definition of entrepreneurship on the basis of risk and inse-curity. Using this concept, it is believed that goods are pri-marily manufactured according to personal motivations and not according to manufacturers' wishes-the manufacturer takes the responsibility of anticipating the buyers' wishes. However, this description of 'entrepreneurs' and their activities was heavily criticized by the Austrian economic school that was led by Schumpeter (1934). Using innovation as a point of entry, Schumpeter proposed that the degree of entrepreneurial inno-vativeness and ability to create goods and services depends on both individual and environmental factors. The environment within which an entrepreneur conducts his/her activities plays a significant role in the entrepreneurship process.

The Definitions of Entrepreneurship in the 20th century

The first definition of entrepreneurship given here was de-veloped in the 20th century. Schumpeter (1934) emphasized the role of innovation and creativity in entrepreneurship. In his in-terpretation of entrepreneurship, all firms which tend to inno-vate tend to introduce one of the following new combinations:

- New products or services
- New production methods
- New markets
- New resources
- New industrial organization

Other than these combinations, there is a school of thought which assumes that entrepreneurship is related to the decision-making process and the development of profitable businesses. This conceptual description of the `essence of entrepreneurship` is believed to be more precise and acceptable than Schumpeter's definition.. However, just like the previous definitions, this definition has certain weaknesses, primarily because it does not include the basic indicators for determining how, and under what conditions, a business activity could be initiated.

To fulfil the gaps identified in the previous theories, a large number of entrepreneurial theorists have attempted to present economic theory based on `rational postulates of human behaviour` after Schumpeter and to synthesize selected theoretical contributions in this area. The works of Casson (1982), is especially distinguished among this group. He criticized the neoclassical economic school for demonstrating extreme subjectivism thus making it difficult for entrepreneurs to anticipate the future. Casson (1982) believes that "entrepreneurs have more relevant information than other people and are always motivated by personal interests".

To expand on his theory, Casson (1982) focused on entrepreneurs' sincere intentions to gravitate towards maximizing profit at a given amount of effort by conducting their business. He argues that the amount of entrepreneurial activity is closely related to the amount of possibilities for making profit. An entrepreneur needs to have a great number of specific personal qualities in order to make a successful business decision. This assertion suggests that specific entrepreneurial qualities such as knowledge, imagination, analytical capabilities, researching capabilities and communication skills are essential. Most of these attributes are explained in this book, except for imagination, which is needs empirical back up.

The debates on what makes a successful entrepreneur is still on the agenda. Other authors have suggested that there are some other entrepreneurial attributes that are regarded as essential in the entrepreneurship process. See for example, Brockhaus (1982), Gartner (1989), Aldrich and Zimmer (1986), Carson (1995) and Delmar (1996) who have stressed that the key psychological characteristics of successful entrepreneurs are: readiness for risk-taking, ambition, optimism, willingness for independence and the need for power. However, other than describing the attributes, which may contribute to an entrepreneur's success, none of the theories have come up with any universal or common attributes of a successful entrepreneur.

The Theories of Entrepreneurship

Having reviewed a number of theories and approaches, it can be argued that there is neither a specific way of defining entrepreneurship nor a way of distinguishing one definition from another. However, the most universal and perhaps, the most acceptable definition is the one given by an American economist, Hisrich (1986). According to Hisrich (1986:26), entrepreneurship is

> "...a process which consists of creating something new which needs time and huge effort, while psychological, financial and other types of risks are taken and material satisfaction is returned".

Other than Hisrich's definition, there are also a number of contemporary approaches that have contributed to the theory of entrepreneurship. For instance, Stevenson and Stahlman (1987) have systematized these theories of the last two hundred years in an excellent manner. They have categorised these theories into three basic groups:

- Theories that regard entrepreneurship as an *economic function*

- Theories that define entrepreneurship from an *individual aspect*

- Theories that define entrepreneurship from a *behaviour aspect*

It is tempting to argue that while some of the theories are inclined towards economic functions, others are based upon researching the individual characteristics of entrepreneurs in an attempt to understand and explain the concept. The former suggests that some of the theories pay more attention to the personal attributes possessed by entrepreneurial people. The researchers' challenge from those theories is, therefore, to identify personal attributes that are unique to entrepreneurs, and to determine those attributes that play a key role in a successful entrepreneur. This approach includes: the psychological, sociological and anthropological aspects of entrepreneurship.

In the newer theoretical considerations of entrepreneurship, Delmar's (1998) theory stresses that earlier behaviouristic approaches are incomplete because they seem to focus on entrepreneurs' attributes that are stable and are not subject to frequent changes. He gave his contribution to the contemporary theory of entrepreneurship - an attempt to integrate economic-psychological models of entrepreneurial behaviour, by developing a model which is based on understanding the entrepreneurial behaviour and environment, as well as determining their influence on entrepreneurial performances (the growth of business and finances). Here is has been suggested that there are different ways of determining entrepreneurial behaviour. It is argued that:

> "...Entrepreneurial behaviour is determined by individual differences like intellectual capabilities, motivation and business characteristics". (Delmar and Davidsson 1998: 165)

For these reasons, the authors represent the view that interpersonal and organizational approaches are very important to the understanding of entrepreneurship. Some contemporary entrepreneurship scientists have attempted to explain small differences between entrepreneurship and marketing. The development of entrepreneurship is likely to influence the development of marketing theory and practices. According to Gartner (1992) differences exist between entrepreneurial and organizational behaviour. Here, it is argued that for an organization to be entrepreneurial, they must somehow posses the ability to relate personal capabilities to the needs of the organization.

Types of entrepreneurship

Based on Gartner's (1986), classification we can distinguish eight different types of entrepreneurship:

1. *Presenting something new* – where businesses are partially started and usually organized between family members and relatives with a low degree of innovating;

2. *Business network development* – businesses are connected through manufacturers, suppliers and distributors (connection of different aspects of business). Everything functions perfectly due to the selection of all participants in performing business activities;

3. *Use of previous experiences, knowledge or business contacts* – in this case an individual has no long-term interest for starting a new business that is connected with business risk. Therefore, individuals often start a business with little capital (usually their personal savings), spending very little time in sales analysis and marketing activities. Instead, they usually use previous experiences, knowledge or business.

4. *Buying a company* – individuals may get interested in buying a developed company for running their own

business. In this case an individual's attention is focused on finding a business with the least business risk;

5. *Conducting expertise* – when an individual is not able to estimate whether a business idea is good for the business or not, this is the approach. In this case, one should hire teams of experts for conducting expertise that should determine and show the validity of a new idea.

6. *Use of services of consulting companies* – an individual (small business owner) may use services of authorized consulting companies when employing and educating employees, giving expert advice related to various areas of business activities, etc.

7. *Special attention focusing on one idea* – in this case emphasis is only on the idea that is not technically specified or is too complex to be easily realized. Regarding the fact that it has special quality, it demands hiring experts and the production of a report. Such expert opinion should be used as a basis for the development of usually, some long term business;

8. *Development of adequate methods of organizing a new business* – An individual (owner) is using various, well-known methods of business planning with the intention to use them as a basis for creating his own method. In addition, he gets to know the necessary details that are important for starting a new business.

Factors that determine the choice of entrepreneurship styles

There is no uniform or universally-accepted form or style of entrepreneurship. Entrepreneurs tend to exhibit unique styles making it difficult to conceptualise this phenomenon. Having listed the classification of entrepreneurs above, there are a number of factors that determine the entrepreneurship styles. However, the type of entrepreneurship styles an entrepreneur decides to adopt depends on the following factors:

- Entrepreneurs' goals when starting the business (company development, tax benefits, working independence, etc.);
- The way an entrepreneur starts – slow (part time engaging) or quick (engaging full time);
- Technological business context (high versus low technology);
- Dependence on company's organizational structure and form of ownership – partnership, franchising, corporative ownership, etc.

Apart from the types mentioned above, the literature offers other alternative types of entrepreneurship such as; buying companies for reselling and many other forms that are explored in the latter chapters.

Gender and Entrepreneurship: Does it matter?

There are a growing number of women who are moving into the private sector and entrepreneurship. However, many researches are still oriented towards men as entrepreneurs. The reason for this can be found in the fact that there are fewer women entrepreneurs compared to male entrepreneurs. However, it can be argued here that women are also capable of forming successful businesses.

Factors that influence the creation of new businesses are different between entrepreneurially-oriented women and men. In particular, this difference is obvious in terms of family and society support, financing sources and problems they are facing (Radović-Marković, 2006). According to the `American Express Small Business Service` research (2002), which was primarily supposed to show similarities and differences between women and men entrepreneurs and managers, it was confirmed that women think differently in terms of conducting business and defining `business success`. Women entrepreneurs see their businesses more realistically and they make attempts to develop them in family environments, while men gravitate more towards developing a business hierarchy with defined rules and working business procedures. A number of theories are based on a feminist analysis, which entails the recognition and analysis of women's structural subordination to men (Calas and Smircich, 1996). In recent years, marketing and financial approaches have also been added.

Due to different approaches to female entrepreneurship, it can be argued here that this field of research is considered to be very broad. Some of the theories outlined in this book can be linked to the study of this phenomenon such as; gender theories, managerial theories, public policy, etc. In our opinion, all of these approaches should be as integrated as possible to be able to provide a complete understanding of female entrepreneurship. In addition, a shift in thoughts and research in the field of female entrepreneurship is also necessary. It should follow the changes in the roles and tasks of women as entrepreneurs that has been largely influenced by new flows of economic operation in the age of globalization (Radović-Marković, 2006).

The recognition of the capacity of women entrepreneurs in our global community is no longer a matter of debate, but is a realisation that female entrepreneurship is now forming one of the major factors contributing to the development of many countries (Radović-Marković, 2007). The defining feature of entrepreneurship in today's global economy is the focus on change in women's lives, particularly for political and economic empowerment that translates into access to financial resources, increased opportunity for education and training, power to affect decisions in their communities, and autonomy in personal life choices.

Chapter 2

THE ENTREPRENEURSHIP PROCESS: GENERATING IDEAS

Business Idea Identification and Business Planning - How can we identify business ideas?

Ideas are the currency of entrepreneurs; therefore, entrepreneurs must play with many ideas to identify the ones which are most likely to bring money and success. But, as a word of caution, it should be noted that not all business ideas contribute to success and profits. Other business ideas are simply unmarketable in some business areas or there might be too much competition already. Therefore, it is important to provide the tools which can either help us to identify the right business ideas and make decisions to either go on to set up and/or not to own a small business.

Find small business ideas that evoke your passion and instigate your creativity

The process of identifying and developing new ideas is a very complex one. The largest number of new ideas is a product of a developed mechanism for potential idea identification. For instance, an entrepreneur asks on every business lunch whether anyone has used a certain product or service. In this way, this entrepreneur permanently investigates the demand and, a possibility for creation of a new product or service. The vast numbers of entrepreneurs do not have formal mechanisms for identifying new business ideas. As a result of such weaknesses, many potential business owners fail to get started.

The sources of new ideas

For most potential entrepreneurs, the hardest part in deciding to set up a business is simply coming up with small business ideas. The most important sources for new ideas are:

Customers – entrepreneurs pay special attention to customers and their needs i.e. they try to test a product or service in an informal way and use the information returned to create an idea.

"...Customers are the only reason your business exists"

Companies – only a few businesses are based on a completely new idea that no one has ever thought of before. Therefore, the best strategy available for most new entrepreneurs is that of using older, tried and tested ideas. Also, by choosing any existing product or service that needs improvement and find a new creative way to approach it and make it better. After all, there are very few products or services that cannot be improved. An existing product or service can be improved by:

- enhancing the quality;
- reducing the cost of production;
- reducing the cost to the consumer;
- improving durability;
- increasing power;
- making it larger or smaller;
- making it more convenient to use;
- making it more comprehensive; or
- updating processes, materials or technology

(See also, Canada Business: Forty Concepts for a small Business, 2008)

When you improve a product, you do not only use the idea from the previous product, but one should seek to improve on it to create a new item.

Copying – this is one of the ways used most often for gathering business information - by analyzing the product and service supply structure, the lack of certain products or services in the market becomes obvious, and that way, an idea is created. An idea is crystallized - this can form the basis for the new businesses and development.

Copying is based on gathering business information

Distribution channels – members of distribution channels are also an excellent source of new ideas. Due to their close connection to the market, members of distribution channels have good suggestions for new products. These members can also be a great source of ideas in marketing, which could be developed later by an entrepreneur. Members of the distribution channels are familiar with the needs of the market and because of that can be excellent sources of new ideas.

Government – the government can be extremely helpful in finding new ideas (for instance, the Patenting Office has countless number of new ideas). Government agencies and government publications can also serve the purpose.

> "...Response to government regulations can come in the form of new product ideas"

Research and development – research organizations represent the greatest source of new ideas, which entrepreneurs later acquire and apply.

> "Primary source of new ideas is research"

One of the meetings in Institute of Economic Sciences, Belgrade where the scientific board discuss new professional and business ideas.

Franchising – This phenomenon is expanded in chapter 11 of this book. It is also one of the options available to women who are thinking of setting-up business ventures. In franchising there is a well-developed business idea, company name, company image, knowledge and experience available from the franchiser. The main advantage of this way of acquiring a business idea is a quick entrance into a developed business.

"...Any good franchise company has developed an idea of doing business that works"

Buying a company – This is also a very common way of starting a new business - individuals can opt to buy a developed business in order to have their own business. Although in this case an individual's attention should be focused on buying a business which has the least business risk.

"... Buying a company that is already established may be easier than starting new one"

Personal experience – In this case, the individuals form new ideas based on previous experience and knowledge.

"Previous experience and knowledge are crucial for new business ideas"

A team of scientists of the Institute of Economic Sciences, Belgrade, Serbia and Faculty of Economics, Ljubljana, Slovenia after the meeting where they discussed opportunities about joint research work in new projects in the field of women's entrepreneurship.

Hobby – A hobby can serve as a source of a new idea – a hobby often grows to a new business, which becomes the entrepreneur's basic business decision.

"...Most people think that working at their hobby would make the best business solution"

Discovering and defining a business idea

It is too risky to set up a business without refining and clarifying your business ideas. The best way to start a business using the idea-generating processes is to set up an appropriate thinking framework. In this context, it is necessary to use all the possibilities of recognizing specific business ideas. If there is a wish for a certain creation that an entrepreneur cannot specify, a business becomes uninteresting and a desire for something new appears. A potential entrepreneur usually says:

"...If only I could get an idea and start a new business. I know I would be successful. I'm a good worker, careful, creative. All I need is an idea. "

There are many business opportunities waiting to be implemented and launched. Maybe the idea an individual is looking for will surface when she is occupied with the other. Sometimes, ideas that may seem quite irrelevant and insignificant or maybe even those that are generated during the resting time can prove to be useful at one point in the entrepreneurs business life. If an entrepreneur likes reading, she may be thinking:

"...What can make my reading more pleasant? What else, besides reading, could I do and what would people like to buy?"

Maybe you would like to make a lamp for a book, or bookstore chain, which has ambient-like private reading rooms. An idea may appear much faster and clearer while an entrepreneur works. For instance, Bette Nesmith, who was a business secretary while on work, before computers and word processors existed, discovered a liquid corrector, which became a revolutionary discovery in typography.

Certain types of business possibilities have no limits. There are possibilities in creating completely new industries (microcomputers and chain restaurants) and in discovering new segments in existing industries (example, pizza home delivery). The key moment in choosing new ideas inside an existing industry is in finding production segments of producing and consuming, which require product or services improvement. It is not necessary to create new market segments; it is possible to become a new competitor inside an existing market segment. If someone was the pioneer it does not mean that it is too late for others to set up similar businesses. The second, the third and the following can learn much from the creator of the market segment and, by applying different strategies and tactics, make even more profit than the first one.

Methods for generating ideas

There are many methods that entrepreneurs can use to generate and test new ideas. The most commonly used methods are:

Brainstorming

Brainstorming method is the best known and the most used for generating ideas. This method is based on the assumption that people can be more stimulated to increase their creativity by meeting other people, and, by participating in developing group experience. An entrepreneur can gather a group of people with whom he/she will discuss and develop new ideas. In this way, many ideas will appear absurd and will not have grounds for further development. Usually one or two ideas stand out. When this method is used, it is necessary to take into consideration certain rules:

a)   Some negative comments are not allowed

b)   As many ideas as possible are desirable – more ideas

mean a better chance for getting to the right one

c) Encouraging, combining and improving ideas is necessary

Focusing on the target groups

This method consists of detailed conversation with a selected group of people. In this method, a researcher focuses on discussion with a group of people in connection with new products. Besides being a good method for generating ideas, it is extremely useful for initiating ideas and new concepts.

Analysis of noted problems

This is another method used for generating new ideas, which is similar to target group method. However, here a customer is offered an entire list of disadvantages of a product prototype. Customers are then asked to identify and categorize problems related to the certain product. Questions are usually about the cost, price, weight, taste, etc. This method is often efficient and useful not only for suggesting new ideas, but also for testing.

Creative problem solving techniques

Creativity is an important attribute for every successful entrepreneur for new product identification and new business creation. However, creativity tends to decrease with age, education, etc. Creativity can be urged in many different ways and by using the following techniques:

a) Reverse brainstorming
b) Gordon method
c) Checklist method
d) Free association method
e) Forced relations method
f) Scientific method
g) Parameter analysis

Every technique listed above will be explained in brief and its use will be demonstrated.

Reverse brainstorming

Accessing the problem in this technique is similar to brainstorming with the difference being that this method allows critics. As a matter of fact, the technique relies on discovering mistakes. This technique should be used as a supplement for other techniques in order to stimulate creative thinking. The process includes identification of everything wrong with the idea. The ways to overcome errors are discussed later on.

Gordon's method

This method relies on the interview of a group of people who do not know the problem's essence. Usually, an entrepreneur starts by providing the general information about the problem. The group of people respond by bringing in/sharing many ideas. Later on, an entrepreneur analyses all the ideas and develops a new concept while maintaining the existing one.

Checklist method

Using this method, new ideas are developed by means of a list of given suggestions. An entrepreneur can use a list of questions, which can serve as sort of a guide for new ideas development. The checklist method may have any form or length.

Free association method

One of the simplest methods for generating new ideas is free association. This technique is useful for the development of a completely new approach to a problem. First, a word or a phrase which is directly related to a problem is examined and later on other words are added, while every word should add something to the previous in order to create a chain of ideas.

Forced relations method

This method represents another technique in a group. The questions about a certain problem are also asked here, with efforts to develop a new idea which would result from the new combination of different ideas and opportunities. A new concept is developed through a process which consists of five phases:

i. Separation of problem elements

ii. Finding relations between these elements

iii. Registering all relations

iv. Analyzing the results of all the new ideas in order to find a good idea or a model development of new ideas from these models.

Scientific method

The Scientific method is widely used in many researching areas. This method is used in observations technique as well as in experimental techniques. The approach includes defining a problem by the entrepreneur, problem analysis, data acquisition and analysis, development and testing potential solutions and the choice of the best solution.

Parameter analysis

This technique includes two aspects – identification of parameters and creative synthesis. Identification of parameters includes variables analysis, thus determining their values. Creative synthesis is developed through developing parameters and relations.

Options analysis

Before one makes a choice from the available options, it is necessary to evaluate the available time, financial resources, expertise, acceptable risk level and financial expectations. Later, the choice of business is made which coordinates the entrepreneur's potential with his expectations in the best possible manner.

Making the final decision

In the process of searching for business ideas, it is necessary to analyze whether those ideas are acceptable and whether they should be implemented. In order to make the final decision, it is necessary to make a serious analysis. The main goal is to find a business which optimally connects the potentials, interests and the entrepreneur's future expectations. It is also important to determine how much time an entrepreneur is ready to spend on his own business. What financial resources are available? If he/she needs additional capital, what are the chances of acquiring it? How skilled is he/she in the new business? What amount of risk is he/she willing to accept? What are the expected financial effects?

It is not unusual to come to a great idea that seems winning and later to find out after business interests analysis; available resources analysis and market analysis, that the idea is not feasible. Entrepreneurs are sometimes in the same position as many big companies that tend to analyze hundreds of scenarios before they make a decision of investing in big projects. However, this should not discourage potential entrepreneurs to set up businesses. The important fact is that business possibilities should be closely examined to provide a realistic picture of expectations and of what the outcome of a new choice. is likely to be.

Our goal is to help potential entrepreneurs to realize that business decisions are much more complex than simply deciding what products or services they will offer on the market.

The issue of time should be primarily examined followed by the financial means needed for starting a business, skill level and acceptable risk levels.

Time factor

Examination of this factor in a business choice context means asking the following questions:

- How much time a potential entrepreneur is willing to spend for his/her own business?
- Will the business allow him/her to accomplish or to maintain the life style he wants or currently has?
- When will the business start to make profit?
- How much time is necessary to defeat competition in the market?

The time planned for development of a business is the main determining factor of the business which needs special attention. Anyone who wishes to develop a business in his spare time needs to opt for a business which demands little engagement. The picture is completely different if *someone* wants to have a full-time business. If one opts for this type of business, there are significant lifestyle differences which one wants to have or maintain during business implementation.

Suppose that a potential entrepreneur decides to open a national restaurant which is open for fifteen hours a day, seven days a week. Having that in mind, a question appears; *will this business compromise his current lifestyle?*

The next problem relates to the amount of time which has to be considered and which is needed for accomplishing potential profit, financial and personal goals. This amount of time varies from a few months to several years, depending on the type of business. It is necessary to have an average time estimate in mind before a business starts. It is especially important with regard to the provision of the financial means during the start-up phase of the business. The amount of time needed for a business to start making a profit is closely related to the matter of competition, competition strength and the ability to suppress them from the market.

Business financing

- How much money is needed for starting a business, providing resources, reserves and procurement of necessary goods, work force employment, settling other operational expenses and covering all life expenses until the moment when a business starts to generate enough money/profit?

- Does an entrepreneur have enough money or credit to provide the initial financial means or does he/she need to borrow from other sources?

- If he/she needs outer financing, will the profits be enough to satisfy potential investors who wish to make certain income returns from capital investments?

Manufacturing and production businesses that often demand significant resources for their start-up can quickly increase significantly. A service business can be started almost without any capital, if an entrepreneur is into personal services (consulting services) and if he/she does not want to invest much in propaganda/marketing or expensive business premises. However, if the service business is a motel or a restaurant, start-up expenses may be very high.

The comparisons stated above are a generalization of this matter. It is impossible to make a conclusion about the necessary financial resources for business implementation because of the large number of factors influencing it. Two persons starting the same business may have completely different start-up investment costs. One will gravitate towards modern equipment, while the other will buy second-hand equipment, thus reducing the amount of investments needed.

Many businesses fail due to the lack of capital available to entrepreneurs. Knowing the exact amount of capital available and possible sources represents a very important factor in starting a new business. Entrepreneurs often think that if they have rented business premises and bought equipment, they have all the conditions necessary for starting a business. Those investments may be the majority of total investments but are far from complete investments. The fact is that not all businesses are profitable at the beginning and some time is needed for a business to "warm up". Sometimes an owner has to borrow capital to secure normal functioning, which means - paying principal and interest on a loan. It is not unusual that even profitable programs get into difficulties because they are unable to pay annuities. Therefore, control is needed: total amount of money borrowed, time of return and interest rate level.

Expertise level

Experience is a very important factor in starting a new business. It is possible to build a successful business in areas where previous experience does not exist. In this case, a risk level is much higher than if certain experience does exist. For those who do not have experience in the chosen business, the risk level can be decreased in several ways. For instance, a business partner or a certain number of employees can be found with particular knowledge and skills, taking the key positions in a company. One could enter franchising businesses or hire consultants who have the experience required for that particular business.

Acceptable risk level

What level of risk is considered acceptable? What level is an individual willing to lose if his business fails? In what ways can risk be reduced or controlled?

Some of the risks related to starting businesses are:

- Development (can an idea be transformed into a product?);

- Production (can a product be economically produced?);

- Marketing (after production, can it be sold?);

- Management (if a product can be sold, is it profitable?); and

- Growth (can business growth be efficiently managed?)

Financial returns

- What are the expectations related to business financial results?

- Will business satisfy entrepreneurs' expectations?

Potential financial results/outcomes is one of the factors to be considered in the decision-making process when starting a new business. However, it is wiser to start a business which is really enjoyed (by an entrepreneur), but which returns only 100 monetary units per year than to get into a business which makes an entrepreneur unsatisfied, but returns larger amounts of money. Bearing in mind what has been said before about factors such as time, money and necessary experience in production, one may ask the question as to why someone chooses a business in which the risk of loss is very high. The reason for entrepreneurs' attraction for it lies in saying *"the higher the risk, the higher the potential profit/returns"*.

Every business has certain limits regarding income and profit. What are some business limits? One of the factors that influence profit potentials is the size of a market. The larger the potential market, the larger the possibilities for increase in sales and profit. Satisfaction in business largely depends on an assumed risk level. This varies from one person to another. Risk itself is also a motivational factor, which inspires action. Many people come to a point where a risk stops any motivation and becomes a destabilizing factor instead. An individual calculates the acceptable risk level and therefore only he knows whether a certain business is convenient or not.

The idea development

Ideas are either drawn from a source of ideas or generated by a creative problem solution; it needs further development and transformation into final product or service.

The development process can be divided into five basic phases:

- Idea phase
- Conceptual phase
- Phase of product development
- Testing
- Product phase

In the idea phase, suggestions are provided for new products or services. The idea, which had passed initial consideration, enters the conceptual phase where it is developed into the elaborated concept with consideration of potential customers' needs. Once the new product concept is developed it is further transformed into a product prototype and tested – product development phase. In this phase, technical and economic aspects are evaluated according to the researcher's specification.

Laboratory testing should be done in the testing phase (pilot products) in order to provide production control and product testing. When it is proved that a potentially new product has better properties than the existing one, then it should be tested further by customers. The development phase results provide ground for creation of a marketing plan. Despite that, it is necessary to run marketing tests in order to assure successful commercialization of products or services. Finally, a business plan should be created in order to test one's own potential business possibilities.

Chapter 3

PLANNING A NEW BUSINESS AND FEASIBILITY STUDY

The advantages of starting a new business

Starting a new business demands extensive research and analysis in order to minimize the elements of business-related risks. This possibility also has advantages and disadvantages and is not different to that of buying an existing or established business.

The main advantages of starting a new business from scratch are:

- Free business positioning;
- Capacities are installed for more efficient use as defined by the business plan and are an original author's idea;
- Innovation possibilities are much bigger if the new business is started from scratch, while all phases of production are created according to the owners' ideas;
- By starting a new business, an entrepreneur creates his own image, which is not the case as in buying an existing company; and
- A new company can be formed with less money, but can still make the same profit as an existing one.

The disadvantages of starting a new business

The main disadvantages of starting a new business from scratch are:

- The high risk involved in starting a new business;
- The long period of time before gaining customers' trust;
- The problem of securing finances for starting a new business; and
- The process of organizing also demands plenty of time in terms of: establishing supply, sales and credit arrangement channels.

Therefore any of the two possibilities stated above has advantages and disadvantages, so none of them is claimed to be an ideal option for starting a business. Some of the advantages and disadvantages can be noticed in advance, which can be crucial for making a final decision or choice. Despite that, before a definitive decision is made to buy an existing business or to buy a new one, it is recommended that a feasibility study is conducted in order to evaluate potential possibilities and limitations.

Feasibility study

Researching with a purpose of creating a new business is much more difficult and so uncertain than research for buying an existing company. Blueprints and results from the past showing how a business evolves are very rare. Feasibility studies are based on numerous analyses and collection of a large number of relevant information for starting a new business, all with the purpose of showing to entrepreneurs whether there is a chance for their business to succeed or not. The issue of potential profit is also explored. In other words, a feasibility study includes collecting, analysing and evaluating information in order to assess whether a business should be started or not. Thus, the question has to focus on those areas which need special attention in order to determine if the chosen idea represents a realistic business opportunity and whether the future entrepreneur knows what he is getting into.

Segments for research of the feasibility study

In order to obtain valuable answers to the question posed above whether *a chosen idea is a realistic business opportunity*, the following segments of research should be covered:

- The choice of business and product name;
- Research into the needs of the product or services which are a part of the processes in the new business;
- Location;
- Market;
- Analysis of material capacities;
- The human resources function needed for running a business; and
- Projection of financial information

The methods and sources for collecting information are numerous and are subject to research by many entrepreneurs and businessmen's guides. Here, we intend to review the information which an entrepreneur should analyze in order to have a realistic evaluation of the potential chances for a company's success. Of course, one should bear in mind the amount of information required for a feasibility study is somehow identical to the number of information needed for evaluation for buying an existing company.

The choice of name

One of the first questions asked when planning a new business is related to the process of determining and choosing a suitable business name. Usually the decision for a name is made quickly, without much consideration or preparation. Most often, the new business is named after the owner or after a member of an owner's family. However, many experts have suggested that this method of choice is a big mistake. There-fore, they recommend planning for this decision. For instance, the choice of name is a long-term decision, which has to be made in relation to the business type the company will conduct and to determine in advance - *why customers are more likely to buy this company's product than others.* To analyse why the rea-sons why customers buy certain products or services, it is ne-cessary to have these questions in such an analysis:

- Product (service) is cheaper than others?

- Product has certain characteristics which other products do not have?

- There is a service at the customers' disposal 24 hours a day?

- Product looks nice?

- Product is well designed?

- There is a high service quality?

- Product (service) has greater value than the price?

Customers' opinions are usually based on emotional rea-sons and subjective judgments. Emotional reasons can be realistic and imaginary. A combination of emotional and ra-tional reasons make the product's reputation or influences the product's image. When an entrepreneur finds himself making decisions on a name, he has to resume all emotional and ra-tional reasons related to the product. For instance, when a cus-tomer hears the name, it has to bring positive associations. However, this doesn't happen overnight. It might take many years to achieve a brand/name recognition of this level.

Ways to choose a name

There are many ways for choosing a name. Based on our re-search we have identified the following:

- Words that do not bring positive emotions particularly those without negative connotations should be used;
- If a word is used that is already in use, it should be tested whether it brings negative emotions with customers;
- Brainstorming sessions can be used, which are organized in friend and family circles. Every suggested name should be individually tested in this case;
- It should be checked if a name that an entrepreneur prefers is being used by another company or product in the same or a similar market;
- Keeping in mind that it is difficult to provoke positive impressions from customers when initials are used;
- It is also necessary to check whether a chosen name represents something negative in some other language;
- It is not wise to consider complicated and complex words because they are hard to remember;
- When the name is chosen, the question is whether it reflects the company's image which an entrepreneur wishes to achieve in the future; and
- A suitable logo should be chosen for the name.

The need for business

Before an entrepreneur starts to realize his business idea, he must determine whether there is a need and a room for his/her business in a certain territory. If there is not enough demand, there is a great probability that a company will not be profitable. Numerous researches are possible, from those on the terrain (why do you buy, where do you buy, which company has the best prices), to those which can use some statistical data (about population per shop at the national level which is a connected to a specific region in which a company is founded). By using the total number of inhabitants in a region, the national average of the number of inhabitants per area, as well as competition strength in the region, it is possible to evaluate the demand for a new business.

Location

An entrepreneur who plans new businesses and who owns a developing business must understand the significance of location for the company's vitality. Among other factors, two are critical to a company's success:

- Analysis of a company's potential residence
- The choice of specific location

These two factors are of extreme importance for a company, which is into retail trade, because of the large competition. Basically, location can be a determining factor when a customer is deciding where to buy (or which store). It should be noted here that, location analysis is more of a dynamic than a static process. It does not stop with establishing a company, but rather continues for as long as the company exists.

Elements for determining business location are:

- Population characteristics
- Competition analysis
- Income level and estimation of population buying capability
- Location accessibility
- Target market structure (age, educational and sex demographics of potential customers)

Market and market analysis

Besides giving answers to previously asked questions related to new business start-ups, preliminary analysis must include many details. Primarily, entrepreneurs must consider the following:

- Are their products or services competitive in the existing market?
- Can their products or services satisfy all the criteria regarding quality in relation to the same or similar competitor's products?
- Is there any reason for not providing required production factors (lack of raw material, energy, expert knowledge, etc?)
- Are sales projections made?

In order to get a precise answer to all the above questions it is necessary to analyze the market by including the following segments of separate questions:

- Determining the potential market;
- Identifying the main competitors;
- Determination of the advantages, as well as weaknesses of the competition;
- Determining the quality and price of other competitive products;
- Impression on customers' competition image;
- Examining promotional activities they use;

Taking into consideration the population volume and structure as being of extreme importance. (of particular consideration should be the trend of population growth, average size of family, income per capita, age, sex and the educational structure of the population. When all the relevant information for market analysis is gathered, an approach is made towards the determination of total sales volume of a target market and its projections. Besides projections, it is necessary to put an advertising plan in place and to determine which media and what dynamics of advertising products and services should be used. Also of extreme importance is the estimation of whether one should expect income from capital and work invested).

In this purpose, the appropriate information should be analyzed and collected, as well as attempt to answer the following questions:

- What are the financial means necessary for starting a business?

- How much profit is expected from a new business?

- How much is the least profit expected?

- How much is the average profit for this type of business?

- What should be done in cases of great business risk and financial loss?

Setting personal goals

When the feasibility study is completed, it should be checked once again to assess the extent of the choice of business and market suitability. At the same time it is important to check if the business suits the interest and desires of the future business owner - *that is, to what extent do personal and market interests overlap?* The most important factor in this phase is to balance personal goals and desires with market demands. To highlight the situation when personal goals harmonize with market demands, we will use a practical example (see Susan's Case study below).

Susan: A case study of entrepreneurial Practices

Susan worked as an agent for a tourist agency for many seasons with great success. She liked the job and wanted to form her own tourist agency which would be intended only for women. The agency would cater for those women who are interested in exotic travel and destinations around the world which always offer something attractive and different. She therefore tried to test her idea by advertising in the `Cosmopolitan`, - a world famous magazine for women. However, her advert didn't get much attention nor did it provoke special interest, so at first she thought that her idea wasn't good and that she shouldn't try to put it into practice. When she was about to abandon her ambition, she turned to an agency for advice and she was given an explanation as to why her advert wasn't successful. Actually, they told her in the agency that "Cosmopolitan" readers are usually young girls in their early twenties who are generally interested in fashion and fashion trends, and are less interested in other things. Therefore the agency recommended advertising again, but this time at the magazine whose readers are women in their 40-ies, which was her target group. She accepted this advice and shortly achieved great success. Thus, she accomplished her intention to be independent in work and to be in the business she wants, but at the same time to be accepted by her market. After she organized the first tour through exotic places in Latin America, Susan published a text in which she pointed out that strong will, persistence, but also consultations with experts helped her to realize her desires. Besides that, she advised all those who wished to start similar businesses to ask for advice from specialized agencies which can provide support, help and to provide an adequate answer to all questions.

Besides agencies which are qualified to help in the way mentioned and are consultative in character, there are more and more women entrepreneurs and manager associations with the basic purpose and goal of providing the necessary information and support for starting a new business. One such association is in Canada (SEA), which is considered to be the largest of its kind.

This association has branches not only in Toronto, but also in other parts of the country. This association has a program developed for women entrepreneurs and managers which is educative and which lasts for ten weeks.

Besides lectures, one can learn from the instructions and share in the experiences of successful women entrepreneurs in this program. On completing the program, during the following year, meetings and consultations continue both within groups and on an individual basis. These and similar programs are offered not only in Canada, but also in the USA and in other parts of the world. When all the necessary information is collected and when the future business owner is about to accomplish a dream, it is necessary to arm her with patience, self-confidence and optimism. Apart from this, she should always have in mind that no success comes overnight as businesses demand a lot of hard work, patience and persistence.

The advantages of setting personal goals

Considering the fact that founding and starting a business can, and usually does influence other aspects of the life of their owners, it is necessary to foresee whether its owner will be able to accomplish some other goals in life alongside business start-up. Therefore, by setting personal goals one can accomplish the following benefits:

- Better organization of life and work;

- Gaining many options and way in life;

- Making better and more rational decisions;

- Higher degrees of motivation;

- Having greater self-respect;

- More peace of mind and more harmony; and

- Doing more for oneself and others.

Although the benefits are obvious when the setting of personal goals is in question, the largest numbers of women entrepreneurs do not define personal goals because many of them do not know whether their personal goals are good and relevant. Some do not know how to check and clarify them. For some, prioritisation is a problem - they do not know how to separate more important from less important goals. For that purpose, some of the numerous tests can be applied and one of them is presented here.

Figure 3.1: *Activity 1:* **The test – How important is your set goal?**

Try to answer as objectively as you can the following fifteen questions:

Is having my own business what I want?

    a) yes   b) no

Did I set my personal and business goals?

    a) yes   b) no

Do my short-term goals fit into my long-term goals?

    a) yes   b) no

Am I able to see through my goal to the end?

    a) yes   b) no

Can I visualize myself in a position where I achieve success and I accomplish my business goal?

    a) yes   b) no

Am I ready to sacrifice for my business and to temporarily put aside some other plans and commitments?

    a) yes   b) no

Am I ready to lose all my savings?

    a) yes   b) no

Am I ready to lower my lifestyle standards in the next several months or years?

    a) yes   b) no

Am I ready to work for 12 or 16 hours a day, six days per week?

    a) yes   b) no

Am I ready to accept criticism and to admit my own mistakes?

    a) yes   b) no

Do I know how to identify and determine less important ideas from the more important ones?

    a) yes   b) no

Do I think that my business success will depend more on myself than on external factors?

    a) yes   b) no

Is satisfaction from running a business greater than financial profit?

    a) yes   b) no

Am I ready, since my business experienced certain difficulties, to continue running it?

    a) yes   b) no

Do I know how to recognize a situation in which I need help and advice from an expert?

    a) yes   b) no

If you answered "no" to some of the questions, then you have to reconsider your goal. Maybe in the short-term this goal will be suitable, but on a long-term basis it will only bring frustrations and conflicts. Therefore, it is always important not only to set short-term goals, but also long-term goals and to see how they fit together. At the setting of those goals (both short and long-term ones), it is important to make the following moves:

- Identify your goals and write them down;

- Write down next to your goal and the date when it should be accomplished;

- State all the problems you will face and you will have to overcome in order to accomplish your personal goal;

- Determine who your associates are, the ones who can help you accomplish your goal;

- Make a list of all the necessary knowledge you should have in order to accomplish your goal (formal educational knowledge and knowledge gained through practice); and

- Develop an action plan which should contribute to a faster realization of the set goal;

It is compulsory to treat *time* as an important factor in running every business and also as an important factor of success. Actually, it is necessary to estimate how much time you need in order to run your own business and then to double that time. Many experts advise those who wish to have a free weekend to "forget" about retail, real estate and service providing businesses. Other than these, there are other activities which are more flexible and do not need the high level of engagement, and can easily fit into one's personal life style.

Making the choice of a business strategy which will be stimulating for employees

It is necessary to determine ways for motivating employees in order to encourage their engagement and to achieve the optimum in a business. In other words, when employees' salaries are connected to their work efficiency, a company will operate well. But what happens when the problem of poor motivation appears or when productivity decreases? In that case, it is of great importance to find the causes as soon as possible. Causes can be numerous and sometimes not easily identifiable. For example, a certain number of employees might think that they are being underpaid, while others seek recognition or better promotion possibilities or better communication with business partners. Therefore, a simple approach such as increasing salary or promotion isn't necessarily the right answer to the situation. Because of this, before an appropriate solution is found, it is necessary to have a conversation with employees and to receive their feedback. Also, many companies tend to hire experts who have holistic approaches and who can provide a complete insight into all the employees' needs and accordingly determine parameters for their fulfilment.

Employees' needs are determined with recognition to their age, work experience, marital status and family size because different benefits appeal to different people since all the employees have different motivations. For example, younger people may be motivated by a company car given to them for their use, while older workers might prefer having a higher status in the company or becoming members of professional associations. The list of professional privileges may be unlimited. We will list only some of them, which could become a part of your program:

- Recreational programs
- Scholarship
- Loans
- Company vehicles
- Profit share schemes
- Legal advice
- Flexible working hours
- Helping employees with childcare
- Extra vacations or prolonged vacations
- Travel at the company's expense
- Paid membership for professional associations
- Establishing special money awards for the most productive employees, etc

As highlighted above, these programs play a pivotal role in increasing work morale and productivity by creating a working environment which will attract, retain and motivate employees. The management's responsibility is huge and is on every level of the organization, in order to transform business from traditional to new forms of work and organizing. Accordingly, managers should create an environment in which people will enjoy their work, be proud of what they do and to always have a clear goal in front of them. Apart from the above mentioned employee motivation techniques aimed at achieving optimal results, we will use an example of the "TD Industries" from Dallas, USA- they tried to value and motivate employees in a specific way., They placed the photos of every employee on the wall - especially those who have been employed for more than five years in the company. Maybe this is one of the reasons why this company is among the most successful one hundred companies in the USA.

In order to create an appropriate working environment, various strategies may be used – "hold", "keep", "seek" and "review". The greatest practical use has "hold" strategy. In this strategy, managers have the main task of motivating and providing support for employees. In order to achieve this, they are expected to be able to create good communication with the employees and to help to eliminate all misunderstandings and negative attitudes amongst staff. By using this strategy of creating an encouraging environment in a company, managers of a glass factory in Indiana conducted a query among employees in order to hear their opinion regarding their working environment and to have an insight into their desires and needs. By reviewing their responses, they came to the conclusion that flexible working hours were the most important factor for the employees. At the same time, this request is one of the most frequently made by employees of companies today.

As this example suggests, employees' demands have to be acknowledged by management in order to achieve the expected business results. In the past several years, 1/3 of managers have changed their opinion regarding the importance of corporate culture and more and more come to the conclusion that the working environment is the most critical factor for "sustaining satisfaction" amongst employees in today's business world. "For many employees, corporate culture is the key determinant in their choice to stay in their organization for a long time" (Smith, 1996). However, only six years before, in the USA, it was thought that the most important factor is the rewarding system (47 % of the examinees among managers put down in first place the importance of a system of rewards, while barely 9 % put working environment).

In other words, companies in the USA today are completely different compared to only half a decade ago and compared to the eighties. There is almost nothing in common between companies then and now. "Culture changes very fast. In the past, it was almost impossible to encourage employees to talk, while today it is enough only to say 'What do you think?' and it bursts. This is an open culture.

In Japan as opposed to the USA, opinion states that managers must spend a lot of time engaging in informal conversations with employees about many problems, even those unrelated to business, has been standard for a long time. All this is done in order to achieve closeness between managers and employees, openness in communication and a desire to work and explore together. Opening communication between employees and managers contributes to the development of a climate of shared responsibility (Whitehill and Takejawa, 1968). Therefore, this is a holistic approach which relies on the strategy of identification of the employees within the company they work for. This strategy is consistent and fits into Japanese culture, which is characterized by its collectivism and desire to avoid uncertainty (Hofstede, 1983). Many experts think that the Japanese combine Western techniques with traditional Japanese attitudes and behaviour which creates flexible and productive working environments (Abegglen, 1958 and 1973; Dore, 1973; Odaka, 1975; Hamani, 1989).

In accordance with previous statements, all business owners are advised to recognize the needs of their employees. Among those needs, the predominant one is the need to reward and to value the contribution of individuals, then to provide employees with the possibility of professional development and permanent education, to enable them to participate in decision-making which is directly related to them and to enable greater responsibility and independence in work for those who want it. By creating a positive working environment and by increasing the level of satisfaction among employees, the best basis for realization of well set working tasks in an efficient and adequate way will be realized. Countries which do not have these changes in the culture will fall behind and will be undeveloped because development is not the matter of technology, or money, or market, but also culture.

Business plan creation

A good business plan has to be developed with the intention to explore all defined possibilities for a business. This is maybe the toughest phase of entrepreneurial process. A business plan is made at the beginning of the year and has to be done professionally, which demands hiring managers and entrepreneurs, as well as a number of consultants or specialized agencies for help. Business plan creation needs more than 200 hours of preparation. It has to be made in a way to give a potential investor a complete picture and understanding of a new business and to enable her/him to clarify important business components, as well as to help him/her to stay on course with his planned business ideas.

Integral parts of a business plan are:

- Production plan
- Financial plan
- Organizational plan
- Marketing plan

The size of a business plan is mostly determined by the amount of means to be invested in planned business. In other words, the larger the amount of means necessary, the more detailed a business plan should be and more estimates and suggestions should be given. Despite that, the realistic average size of a business plan is between three and ten pages of text, which accents the most important business details with related financial estimates.

The use of Microsoft (MS) Project in entrepreneurship and management for business plan creation

The use of Microsoft Project tools should contribute to easier estimates, analyses, and project evaluations. Their task is also to help to correct while working or to change complete goals and tasks set in a project if they do not appear to be appropriate. Thus the risk is reduced as well as the possibility of making bigger mistakes, which consequently reduces expenses, influences the higher utilization of resources and optimizes time use. It is necessary to make a list of project priorities and set hierarchically tasks and goals in order to track activities and to control project effects. Also, in order to get a realistic picture of a project, it is necessary to integrally recognize the relevant financial indexes. This is very important because of the relevant valorisation of financial profitability and the profitability of investments in certain projects. This includes determining what useful information is required for making the right decisions related to the financial position and success of a project. In order to achieve this, it's necessary to train managers.

The training process should provide appropriate instruments and techniques for every management level. Every one of them should learn organizational process for project management. One of the best ways to do that is by giving project managers corresponding manuals in which explain in detail what and how project managers work. After the training, every management level should enter business with new set of knowledge and skills for practical work on project. Education and training should include not only project managers, but also all employees, so everyone can gain the knowledge necessary for the job. Righty, it is then expected that all team members will have the appropriate knowledge in order to make use of the great possibilities provided by Microsoft Project 2007, i.e. how to use its tools in order to make the greatest effect. Above all other things, they are expected to know:

- That MS Project is an extremely powerful calculator – it has a huge number of possibilities and options for different types of calculations

- As many detailed tasks as possible should be inputted to take into consideration all the facts available. The more a manager knows about his own project, the more detailed will be the working tasks defined. Also, he may divide work tasks into a number of subtasks in order to monitor them more easily. In that case, MS Project automatically focuses on set tasks by putting them in Summary task.

- A situation should be created in which every individual involved in the project knows in advance how his work will be evaluated before it even starts.

- For every part of the project, a budget should be determined, as well as a working program and conclusion time. Also, measurement units must be determined according to what success can be evaluated on project completion – this enables easier and faster problem solving than in usual situations, where normally, at the end of the project a team meeting is held in which the team determines where the problem has appeared and how it should be handled.

- They have to know to make a strategic project – they are put in relation with business results evaluation and the goal is to analyze business situation and to build a network of business achievements.

- It is needed to make project protocol - organizational protocol for project management which describes the executive, program manager, and project manager roles. These roles demand specific information flow and decisions in every one of these three levels.

- With help from MS project tools, to provide a consistent system of planning it enables project executives to:

  a) Compare expenses and incomes

  b) Efficiently allocate many resources and people to projects.

- When the plan is finished, weekly reports and MS Project are used to determine what has happened and what was expected and if there are any problems to offer adequate solutions.

- Project plan creation for every team member- these plans which are based on the results of every team member, are meant to determine individual achievements, but also mistakes. The result is that everyone knows how they work and what can be expected if they do not work well.

Thanks to Microsoft Project 2007, the ability to keep a huge quantity of information is provided; it's easier to keep track of work dynamics, realization levels of set work tasks, expenses and others, all of which make the company more competitive. In this way, it helps to find those methods which contribute to achieving the best internal and external company performance. It indirectly influences the change of company's organizational structure thus stimulating it to restructure into a more functional and more efficient company. Therefore, with new management models, a higher degree of efficiency when making business decisions is provided. Therefore intensifying information technological development and increasing the use of software as basic instruments of modern business are every country's imperative.

Chapter 4

STARTING A BUSINESS

Motivational factors of women in making decisions for starting small business

Although women, like men, when starting their own businesses are led by a desire to achieve success, they still show different motivation for getting into the business world. There are also some other important differences which distinguish women from men in this profession. The following are the most dominant:

1. Women start businesses in order to accomplish flexibility, independence and to free themselves from corporative boundaries. Besides that, many women look for personal satisfaction through running a business independently and to create space for advancing in a career. Also, one of the basic motivational factors which move women in starting their own business is in the creation of a safe future and the possibility of a choice of lifestyle and work style.

2. Women are often motivated to start their own business because of the dissatisfaction with their status in their jobs and because they feel that they advance much slower in their career than men and also that they can never achieve the position which belongs to them by their expert and other qualities.

3. More than half of women owners (53 %) are guided by intuition when they start and run a business, while men (71 %) are guided only by logic.

4. Two thirds of women (60 %) compared to male business owners, examine all possibilities before they make a decision and start some action. They also tend to gather information from their consultants and entrepreneurial associations more than men do. They tend to successfully weigh up every possibility and to balance different tasks and priorities.

"There are significant differences between women and men entrepreneurs"

Women entrepreneurs' profile

- Willing to take risks
- Have a high level of energy
- Have a high level of personal motivation
- Have an average work experience of nine years in business
- Are mostly married and have a father who is an entrepreneur
- Have good communication skills
- Have general managerial knowledge and skills
- Spend between 35 and 50 hours per week on the job
- Have a tendency to quickly make a profit

Business entities

When a business idea becomes clear and when a future entrepreneur decides whether he/she likely to buy an existing business or start a new one, then the next step expected is to determine the legal and organizational form for the company.

Legal Forms

There are different business entities and legal forms including:

- Companies based on individual ownership
- Partnership
- Corporation

All three forms are different and can be compared in terms of ownership, starting expenses, continuity, profit distribution and attractiveness for investment. In order to notice the similarities and differences of these three forms, it is necessary to make a comparative analysis.

Legal possibilities

- *Individual ownership* - Total freedom to sell or transfer to anyone any part of a business
- *Partnership* - Main partner may transfer only his part of the business and only with approval of other partners. Other partners may sell their part without the other's approval
- *Corporation* - Stakeholders may buy or sell stocks as they wish. Some forms of stock transferring may be agreeably limited.

Collecting capital:

- Individual ownership - Capital can be provided through crediting of owners increased contribution;
- Partnership - Credit or new contributions demand changes in the partnership contract;
- Corporation - New capital is collected either by selling actions or bonds or by taking loans for the corporation.

Management control:

- Individual ownership - Company's owner makes all decisions and can act promptly;
- Partnership - Credit or new contributions of partners, demands changes in the partnership contract;
- Corporation - New capital is collected either by selling actions or bonds or by taking loans for the corporation.

Profit and loss distribution:

- Individual ownership - Owner is the only one responsible for business success or loss, accordingly he takes all the consequences;
- Partnership - Distribution depends on the contract between partners, as well as on invested capital;
- Corporation - Stakeholders may distribute profits through dividends

Attractiveness for collecting capital:

- Individual ownership - Depends on the owners capabilities and business success;

- Partnership - Depends on the partner's capabilities and the amount of invested capital;

- Corporation - More attractive as an investing possibility because of the owners' limited responsibility.

Family Support for starting and running entrepreneurial activities

It is desirable for a woman who wishes to start her own business, besides determination of her own affinities, to hear family opinions. Having support from the family can be a good ground for achieving success, especially when the family is included in the decision-making or problem solving processes. Sometimes it is good to employ certain family members and trust them with some jobs for as long as conditions are not appropriate for engagement of outside employees, that is, as long as the company is not on a solid ground. In that way, certain corrections of ideas are possible at the very start and also you get the harmonization of business, personal and family goals.

However, different from other environments where the family is supportive for a woman and man in this type of initiative, there are other extreme cases in which big conflicts arise in families, which in the most drastic ways may end up in divorce. Having this in mind, a recommendation for all prospective entrepreneurs is to test their families and to consider their answers well, because they can sometimes be a touchstone whether they should quit the idea to start to own a business or not.

Figure 4.2: *Activity 2* – Do you have sufficient support from your family?

Did you inform your family about the idea of starting a business?

Yes   No

Does your family have a positive attitude towards women who engage in entrepreneurial and managerial businesses?

Yes   No

Is your family ready to help you in every way (material and moral) if necessary?

Yes   No

Is your family capable of supplying childcare or support during your absence?

Yes   No

Can your family accept the fact that due to business investments it can expect a decrease in the family standard, maybe even for a longer period?

Yes   No

Does your family agree to taking a bigger loan and to have a mortgage on a family house completely aware of all the implications of this decision?

Yes   No

If you have positive answers on most of the questions, it means that you have all the conditions necessary to move forward.

Five most common mistakes, which are made at the start of business

Although there are a number of factors, which can influence a bad choice of business, the following are the five most characteristic mistakes:

Mistake 1: Hobbies are mostly transformed into small businesses not taking care whether there is a demand on the market for specific types of products or services;

Mistake 2: The business is started without adequate planning or creation of business plans.

Mistake 3: A huge number of entrepreneurs avoid consulting experts when choosing a business to go into, whether this is because they think that they know everything there is to know or that they expect to be lucky is unclear. Many of them rely only on intuition which although is of great significance, is not enough. On the other hand, it would be more desirable to consult not only with experts, but also with those who already own companies with a similar business orientation. It is useful that future entrepreneurs work in such companies for a while, as they have the experience which could inspire their new businesses, thus gaining necessary knowledge and experiences. By observation of the best, one can avoid many business traps, and minimize unnecessary expenses and losses. Learning not only from one's own example, but also from others can also be useful in elimination of mistakes which will not be repeated in their future businesses.

Mistake 4: When they make a final choice of business, many potential entrepreneurs neglect the importance of determining whether the selected business will be profitable or not and to what extent. In other words, thinking about whether ideas about a certain type of business present a realistic business opportunity and whether an entrepreneur knows what he/she is getting into. For that purpose, a feasibility study must be used, which will contribute to the starting-up of businesses not only because of the existence of desire and affinity for a certain type of business, but also because of the objective possibilities for the business to succeed.

Mistake 5: Many entrepreneurs enter into business without knowing in advance the time necessary for organizing and running a business. Very often it happens that new businesses make themselves more engaged than the time available to do so or are willing to spare. Therefore, it is suggested that during the first six months of running a new business, they solely devote to business and to subordinate all other activities to the business.

In order to avoid these mistakes, personal goals should be carefully examined and thought through and then turn to the business idea with the intention to estimate whether it fits into business and life frames and whether it can contribute to work and life flexibility.

Before making a decision to start a business, it is necessary to check what is necessary and what motivation we have behind the intention. In other words, apart from the desire to own a business, we should ask ourselves: *do we own certain tendencies for starting and managing our own business?* For these reasons, it is recommended that every aspiring entrepreneur should attempt to answer the following questions as objectively as he/she can, in order to use test results as a specific road map to establishing whether or not he/she should embark on setting up a business.

Figure 4.3: *Activity 3* – Test whether you have the affinity for starting your own business?

I have a strong need to succeed in business
    Yes   No   Maybe
I have a strong desire for self-proving
    Yes   No   Maybe
I am very intuitive
    Yes   No   Maybe
I always want to explore and to learn something new
    Yes   No   Maybe
I am self-confident
    Yes   No   Maybe
I always do work in my own way
    Yes   No   Maybe
I like to take risk
    Yes   No   Maybe
I'm enterprising enough to start my own business
    Yes   No   Maybe
I want to run my business alone and to make business decisions
    Yes   No   Maybe
I see problems as challenges
    Yes   No   Maybe
If I want something, then it is always on my mind
    Yes   No   Maybe
I have many business ideas
    Yes   No   Maybe
I am persistent at work
    Yes   No   Maybe

I am capable of finishing work on time
    Yes   No   Maybe
I easily adapt to variable business conditions
    Yes   No   Maybe
I enjoy competition
    Yes   No   Maybe
I know many successful women entrepreneurs
    Yes   No   Maybe

> I read business literature and I collect various information
> Yes   No   Maybe
> I'm in good psycho-physical health
> Yes   No   Maybe

Instructions for using the test:

If your answers on most of the questions were "Yes", it means you have the potential to start the business and to succeed in it, but besides that, you have to work on improving your own skills and knowledge in all areas where you express weaknesses. If "Maybe" was your most frequent answer, it means that you are very indecisive and that starting on your own business could prove to be challenging, but instead you need to find partners for your venture. Partners in business are necessary in order to supplement each other in various fields of your business. Negative answers mean that you should not abandon the idea to start your own business, but take time and give it another look. The other options available would be to be employed in some of the existing companies or to work for others until you have improved your confidence in business. In any case, you are the final decision-maker! Therefore, you should judge for yourself and make a final decision.

Useful tips which should be followed in making the choice of the right business

1.   Start the business you like, not exclusively the one that can bring you huge profit, although you don't have enough affinity for that type of business;

2.   Select the business suitable for your knowledge, experience and interests;

3. Determine the strategy of management, as well as the location and conditions in which the business will run (a company located outside home or in the home);

4. Make a selection and train the personnel;

5. Determine how much investment you need for starting the business and be obliged to spare funds for a feasibility study;

6. Consider the fact whether you can run the business on your own and to take full responsibility and risk, or whether you need to share all that with someone else;

7. Determine how much engagement on work you need daily;

8. Be optimistic, but also realistic in setting goals;

9. Start reading expert books and magazines on business in order to get some new ideas which could be useful;

10. If you have certain doubts or you need advice from an expert, you must consult experts in management and entrepreneurship. It costs much less than future mistakes if a potential business owner runs his own experiments without having enough knowledge or experience in that domain. It is not always best to learn by your own mistakes.

Chapter 5

THE CHARACTERISTICS OF BUSINESSES THAT ENTREPRENEURS DO FROM HOME

Introduction

In record numbers, women are breaking out of corporate life and embracing entrepreneurial careers as an alternative to the "glass ceiling". Female entrepreneurship is realizing its potential as we witness women emerging as business owners in economic sectors they have not previously occupied. Businesses that entrepreneurs do in their homes are relatively new. Those are usually smaller businesses in the field of providing intellectual and other services. According to many indexes, these businesses are very stable, which is affirmed by data that the average age of businesses which owners run from their homes is around six years. Also, according to research of the "National Foundation of Women Business Owners" (1997), women business owners who work from home are much more likely than other women business owners to use credit cards and personal means for financing their businesses. They generally do not wish to depend on loans and credits. For example, only 12 % of women home business owners during 1994 in the USA used commercial loans, while in the same year, as much as 40 % of women used credits and commercial loans for running businesses outside their homes.

The research also showed that women who work at home use computers and modern technology more than in other types of businesses, more than 565 of them use computers for everyday tasks. Two thirds own a fax machine, 55 % use cellular phones, and 30 % have a CD-ROM and 32 % use the internet. In this way, by opening the door to modern technology and by using it in every day work, women gained more opportunities in choosing business which best suit their lifestyles.

Sixteen rules for running a successfully business from home

It is not easy to work from home, although it seems so at the first sight. With increased costs of business premises and needs for flexibilities, many people have a vision of setting up businesses in their homes, which should provide plenty of time for rest, socializing, dealing with family and other personal activities. They expect that in this way, they will avoid long business meetings, boss' critics if they are late for work etc. However, although working from home allows more freedom and different opportunities for the quality use of time, still business owners fall into traps. Some lack organizational capabilities and fail to structure their commitments and time. In order to succeed in business intentions and to avoid the traps of running business at home, we are going to list several rules which should be followed:

a) **Follow your heart** – Energize your entrepreneurial idea by initiating it and turning it into solid activities

b) **Services** – Think of how your business will be unique and think of an original way of maximizing the service for clients and customers

c) **Customers must always have your full attention** – It is well known that every business is born with a product or a service and that it dies without customers. Therefore, no matter what type of business you start, whether it is e-business or traditional, it is important to maintain control of all its operations and resources. Among these, customers are considered the greatest source of all. Therefore, connect with your customers and offer them a reason to come back to you. From these reasons it is very important to create a positive experience for them, which is the combination of everything a customer sees and in takes part in. Always have in mind that customers' positive experiences are key to the success of every small business

d) **Emphasize your uniqueness as compared to others** – Find a market which doesn't have a high level and quality of services and offer something new and original. For example, instead of a simple offer of secretarial services, offer those services which will improve the development of small businesses at home.

e) **Become a technical fanatic** – Use the advantages of the latest technical-technological instruments, which should help your business to improve and develop. Permanently innovate and redesign your web presentation and work on it in order to make it more interesting for a greater number of visitors.

f) **Connecting** – Connection to the external world over the internet is essentially important, as well as connecting through professional associations, organizations and the like. If you are afraid of the idea to individually run your business from home, partner with another business women or find more partners. More and more women lately are forming partnerships in order to work together.

g) **Structure your time** – It is necessary to observe good time management to avoid mixing private with business commitments.

h) **Group your jobs** – Try to minimize the time you spend outside your office during time that has been dedicated for work.

i) **Use the services of experts and practice team work** – Business owners think that they can keep everything under control and usually they relate to the business as overprotective parents. Actually, they think that no one can do a job better than themselves. Such a relationship may be a limiting factor for further growth and business success. Therefore, it is necessary to form a team of experts and external associates who will have a critical approach to business and which will be more objective than the owner. Monthly meetings with associates are recommended, where all business opportunities, challenges and potential mistakes could be discussed. Accordingly, a correction of the business plan or feasibility study is also recommended, when necessary. Changes are considered real in any project situation. They are desirable in every segment or element of a project. In order to initiate them, all circumstances should be considered, all changes and so are other variables. Also, associates' opinion should be considered because they are the carriers of the new ideas, they recognize mistakes, give suggestions and opinions. Therefore, whenever this is possible, opportunities for corrections and changes should be accepted on every project. Actually, the basic idea is not prevention of changes, but the control of changes. This is the basis of managing changes in a project. Entrepreneurs should consider two basic types of changes:

i. *Reactive changes* – those which are necessary in order to respond to project problems (technical errors, the lack of resources, etc.)

ii. *Requested changes* – These changes may arise from new ideas, new information or new business perspectives.

j) **Control your project and the level of realization of your business plan** – Every efficient way of project control has to rely on four basic elements of management of the changes:

i.   What types of changes are allowed?

ii. How will the changes be shown?

iii. In what form will changes be requested?

iv. How will the changes be incorporated into the business plan?

We shall consider individually every one of the above four elements.

i. What types of changes will be allowed?

With the intention to control the changes of any project, it is necessary to determine the limits of the problem, that is, to determine the types of changes which may be allowed. However, without doubt, those changes which should lead to saving and the survival of a project must be accepted.

In order to accept efficient limitations, changes in every individual sector, it is necessary to consider several factors:

- **Value and priority** – if a project is important, it may be requested that changes are limited to a degree to avoid unwanted risk.

- **Time** – if changes are requested in the early phase then they can be implemented early, which is not the case if a project has entered into the second phase of its realization.

- **Expense** – project changes can reduce or increase its expenses. Therefore, it is recommended that a special fund is created for covering expenses increased by project changes.

ii. How will the changes be shown?

When a request for a change in a project is sent, it has to be recorded under a specified number and shown with detailed definition of the complete structure of changes which should consist of the time dimension of corrections, expenses and types of changes. It should also be determined who is responsible for changes; is it a business owner, a project manager or team of experts.

iii. In what form will changes be requested?

It is important for the form in which requests for changes should be presented (written form, oral form, email, etc.). Who has the authority to request changes? However, regardless of what form it is presented, every request must contain the following information:

a. Project name

b. Name of person who sends the request

c. Date when request is sent

d. Description of changes

e. Signature of person who sends the request

iv. How will the changes be incorporated into the business plan?

When the request for changes is sent and the desired changes on a project are listed, then it comes to incorporating those changes into the business plan of a project whose realization is in progress. Depending on the specific type of change, that is whether it relates to a single or several project elements, it is necessary to make a revision of project plans, technical design, budgets and project documentation.

In order to incorporate project changes seamlessly into the business plan and to provide positive results in the future, it is necessary for project managers to have special knowledge and skills. Actually, their role is the most significant; having in mind that management of change is a very risky and sensible process which demands a combination of planning and communication skills, logical and creative capabilities, work experience, etc. These skills are necessary regardless of the type of project in question and the level changes applied. Therefore, it is always recommended for business owners to apply project changes in coordination with the project manager or to completely rely on the project manager.

Manage your project documentation efficiently

Project documentation provides the necessary information, has all the ideas and is a solid basis for making business decisions. Actually, all key elements of a project are incorporated in basic documents. Therefore, managing the documentation of a project is extremely important for that project's success.

What is management of project documentation?

Project documentation management is defined by practice and procedure which includes creation, distribution and the keeping of various types of project documentation.

The goals of managing project documentation

Basic goals of the management of project documentation are:

- Creation of mechanisms of control of the project documentation;
- Provision of standard forms;
- Minimizing errors; and
- Ensuring that all documents are gathered and distributed on time.

In order to accomplish these goals, it is necessary to provide appropriate instruments which vary from the simplest to the most complex which are in the basis of every system of project documentation management. The system of project documentation management must contain the following elements:

- **Input:** Means by which documents will be created and distributed. Project documents may be created by the project team, but can also be obtained outside the project team.

- **Documentation review:** Gathered documentation is reviewed by a team of experts and specifically shown to the whole team of associates on a project.

- **Control version:** Means by which project changes are recorded during a certain time interval and are documented.

- **Output:** Determining how to present the documentation which should be distributed (by email, printed material or some other acceptable form).

- **Research:** Determining how to analyze gathered documentation (by using specific information or by keywords).

- **Documentation archiving:** Determining how the documentation will be kept and used later in case of need. Every project must, regardless of its size, have a coordinator; a person who will be responsible for project documentation. Depending on the volume of the documentation, such a person may be engaged either full time or part time as an associate. However, regardless of how they work, the coordinator's role is always the same. Actually, his responsibility must relate to the following field of his employment:

  • To determine and to identify the project's requirements and to, accordingly, determine a procedure for gathering project documentation;

  • To enable support and help for all project team members;

  • To determine which type of project documentation is needed, considering project plans, contracts, technical documentation, work specification, reports, etc.

- How and when gathered documentation will be used;
- Who will enter the data onto prepared forms;
- How will the documentation be applied and used depending on the complexity and the size of the project;
- To determine the standards of documentation gathering according to technical capabilities and depending on the complexity and the size of the project;
- To determine which software will be used for different types of documents;
- To determine the format of each document;
- To define how documents will be classified by their importance;
- To determine how the documents will be distributed;

At the end it can be said that the responsibility of the project documentation coordinator is great and that it varies depending on the requirements, goals and tasks of a project. However, the common thing for all coordinators to note is the fact that they must define the required documentation in time, to secure its gathering and distribution, as well as to make it available to the owner and all associates and end users.

Getting started at home

Having gained the necessary knowledge and techniques, now it is time to put your ideas into practice. The following steps will seek to enable you to set up your home business by considering both physical and intangible resources available:

Determine what part of your home you can dedicate as your office

It is desirable to dedicate a part of your home as a separate space in which you carve out everything you need for running a business.

Determine how much money you need for founding and development of a business and how to provide it

There are three ways of providing the money, after you make a financial plan, which has all financial estimates and necessary indexes:

- personal means
- loans
- investors

Here, one must have in mind that the best way for founding a home based business are personal means, because the chances of finding investors for this type of business or obtaining a loan are slim, as long as these businesses don't prove themselves successful.

Select the legal form of company which suits you best

Consult your lawyer, accountant or other experts to give you advice on legal matters, in particular the type of legal form your company should adopt based on your current situation. In doing this, one should take into consideration:

- Taxes to be paid (and their calculations)
- The amount of disposable money available
- Family structure and their participation in the business
- Contacts with potential partners
- Business development plans
- Customers
- The number of employees

Acquire licenses and permits

One must not start the business without appropriate licenses for founding a company, regardless of whether the business is run from home or not. A number of business owners think that they do not need a license for their business because they are based at their homes. This is a wrong concept. It is important to be at the right end of the law.

Collect the necessary information

Some business tasks are the same for all types of small businesses, while others are different and specific for business at home. An entrepreneur should have this in mind when he/she organizes their business. Actually, apart from hiring an expert for certain fields of business, careful planning and information gathering, based on conversations with a number of private home business owners can be very helpful for appropriate business management – establishing working discipline, rational use of all available resources, less time and energy spending, etc.

Provide the necessary knowledge for running a business

Many people have good business ideas, but lack the knowledge on how to make them successful in business practice. Managing an activity means having the ability and mind skills which are essential for success in every field of life. Managing a business is a skill of its own, which requires much knowledge, techniques and experience, and above all, their successful integration into the whole, which should lead to the optimal use of human and financial resources in order to achieve business results. To achieve this, various software tools are used around the world, which should serve managers well for the purpose of estimating the validity of planned tasks, their well-timed correction and the reduction of unnecessary expenses due to the irrational use of planned time, the inadequate use of resources and other business mistakes. In this way, easier risk management is achieved, as well as the reduction of possible errors.

Four common mistakes made at the start of a home business

Home businesses, just like any other forms of businesses are not immune to problems. There are a number of factors that could lead to failure. However, some of the mistakes can be avoided or minimized. We have listed a few. These include:

Insufficient market

The main reason for home businesses failure is an insufficient market. A great number of entrepreneurs start their business with a careless attitude about whether there is a demand for their products or services. Sometimes they learn this at the very beginning of running their business and sometimes they learn this too late, after they have spent a lot of money, effort and time on the business.

Determination of the level of a demand is sometimes preliminary market research which is necessary. If there is a lack of money and a complete research cannot be conducted, then it is necessary to make conversations with owners of similar businesses in the same economy branch, suppliers, and experts from economic chambers, even with potential customers, in order to test a market for business. The most important thing is to collect as much business critical information as possible. When one determines that there is no demand for products or services, the best course of action is to make a revision of business plans as soon as possible and to redefine business strategies. It is expected that an experienced and knowledgeable entrepreneur knows how to reduce losses and to quickly react and make a turn in business.

Bad operational management

The majority of home business owners think that time should not be lost on maintaining statistics, neither is it of any use to observe various indexes of business activities as time functions. Instead, they pay more attention to market expansion or new business strategies development. However, practice proved that one should not neglect the observation of business activities trends, where one can easily see certain weaknesses and losses from the past. This is often an excellent road map for what should be changed in future.

Mistakes in signing business agreements

A great number of business owners make mistakes in signing agreements which are not supported by written contracts. For them, the most convenient way of making business agreements is using verbal agreements and therefore, if certain changes are made or agreements broken, there is no legal basis for one of the sides to seek legal protection at the court of law. This situation is the most common in business partnerships. Basically, some studies show that a half of business partnerships in the world are made without formal written agreement. It looks much like a marriage without a contract, that is, it may have many advantages, but little legal protection. Possession of written document is the best protection that can be obtained in business.

"Try to find me"

A number of entrepreneurs think that customers will find them easily and that they shouldn't take care of customers. However, this opinion is completely wrong regardless of where the business is located – in the city trade centre or some other distinguished places. It is necessary that entrepreneurs meet customers, not to wait on them passively. This is especially important for business over the internet, where a web site is not a guarantee that customers will be easily attracted. Therefore a promotion of business is recommended, advertising, different types of presentations and the like which should turn the attention to business itself.

How do you determine whether a business organized at home is on the road to success?

It is logical to expect that everyone who starts a new business wishes it to succeed, regardless of the type of business and the way it is organized and run. But what does it mean to be successful in business? As an entrepreneur, this is a question which you are expected to ask yourself, having in mind that you spend your energy, time and money, as well as talent to create a new business. Actually, despite all your efforts, experience and knowledge, sometimes it may seem that your business is not going the way you want or as you expected. Therefore self-evaluation is important as it should be a part of your daily management process. Learning how you work may be an excellent basis for deciding which way to go next. There are several tests which can help in determining how good or bad your business is. One must have in mind that the success of a five year lasting business cannot be evaluated in the same way as one that has been up and running for only for six months, - practically in the phase of development.

Some ways of determining the road on which the business is heading:

Have you achieved all planned goals?

Compare your business plan with your results. Also compare performances of your business to other competitors. Determine your share of the market

Do you pay your bills regularly?

One of the main indicators of your business success is whether you are in a position to cover your expenses on time and to pay your duties and taxes. If you are, you may consider your business as a good functioning one. If you are not able to fulfil these commitments, then it is necessary to take certain steps and to make additional efforts to improve your business activities. Maybe the only thing you have to do is to decrease your expenses or maybe your choice of business was wrong. Also, do not expect that you can make a lot of profit during the development phase, it takes time and you have to be patient. The advice for all those who enter entrepreneurial waters is to be patient and to do their work well and qualitatively. If you work in this manner, in the long-term your business will certainly meet your material and other expectations.

Have you done more as an entrepreneur or when you were employed by someone else?

Many entrepreneurs start their own business because they are not satisfied with their current job, material and social status. Therefore, when you enter entrepreneurial waters, it is necessary to ask yourself whether you earn more now compared to a period when you were working for someone else. Also, it is desirable to compare earnings of your colleagues who run similar businesses, have similar education and work experience as an entrepreneur similar to yours. All these answers will provide an excellent index to show you whether you are more successful now than in the previous job when you were employed by someone else It is also important to evaluate the making of a decision about what to change in your professional plan for the future, that is, whether the existing business should be modified in some areas or replaced with some other, will depend on these answers.

What does a financial report show?

A simple financial ratio analysis is the best way to show financial weaknesses and advantages of your business

How are the sales doing?

It is necessary to examine the trend of the sales of your products by comparing the data with previous months and previous years. If you notice a constant decrease of your sales, you must stop and make a different sales strategy. Actually, these data should show whether your marketing efforts are efficient; do the distribution mechanisms operate well and is there still an expressed demand for your products or services.

Are you making profit?

Do you lose or earn money? When can you expect profit from your business? Do you have sufficient financial means to cover expenses and losses while your business is without profit? In the long- term, is you business profitable at all?

How do you feel about your business?

Maybe the answer to this question is one of the best indicators as to whether you have achieved business success or not. Actually, many entrepreneurs start their business from different motives. Some of them were already mentioned, but the one which is of extreme importance is whether the business is approached with the same passion as in the beginning? At the end of this analysis you may conclude, without a consultation from an expert, whether your business is worth your engagement and effort. Only the business which fulfils you in every way and makes you happy can bring you success.

The most common problems in running home businesses and the ways for overcoming them

Taking care of family; raising children and running a business at the same time are two serious jobs which need full-time engagement. Therefore the everyday schema of commitments is overloaded with numerous activities. Numerous problems and frequent mistakes appear which may negatively reflect on business success in total. Among the most frequent are:

Family conflicts

Family conflicts are a frequent phenomenon because of an inability to balance family and professional commitments, which often faces no understanding among family members. Actually, when someone works at home, working space is immediately close to other rooms where other members of the family spend their time, which may bother both sides. These conflicts will be smaller if there is family harmony and understanding of all family members. A home business owner should explain to family members that (if they are not in that business themselves) during the day, some time must be dedicated solely for professional causes. The family must agree with the owner to work longer than working hours during the first several months in the first business phase. After that initial phase, which is always the toughest for any business owner, working hours may be gradually shortened, or external help may be obtained. It is extremely important not to ignore this issue. If it is ignored, it may cause even greater problems, in both the business and family – which is bad for both sides.

It is desirable to spend an hour or two exclusively for family matters and to turn off the fax machine at that time, not to answer telephone calls and not to think of business at all.

Separating professional and family life

Many entrepreneurs, who run businesses at their homes, consider permanent contact with their family a great advantage in running a business. However, apart from its good sides, it can be a huge disadvantage. Above all, daily home commitments may easily take over the time of professional commitments and regular activities (for example, answering mail, sending fax messages, e-mails, etc.). In other words, many entrepreneurs who opted for working from home have problems organizing themselves. Considering that they often mix private with professional commitments, they make one of the biggest mistakes when it comes to running a home business. This can be explained by the fact that, being a boss to oneself is a lot harder than it may seem. Many do not even have experience of running a business as as individual and, for some it is their first time and therefore, they use their time irrationally and have a lot of idle time. It is recommended for all those who are inexperienced in this matter; to obligatorily plan their working activities and commitments, both in the long-term and daily.

Not having a dedicated working space

Having a home office is not a problem if there is sufficient space for it. However, if this is not the case, then it is necessary to have at least some space at home to put a desk, computer and equipment for running a business. It is important to separate working space from living space.

Not having a dedicated phone line

Often the same telephone number is used for both private and professional purposes. Instead, it is necessary to have a dedicated telephone line for the office in order to appear more professional. Phone calls should be answered as polite and patiently as possible, in order to make a good impression to customers.

Bad image of the business –

Many entrepreneurs, who have developed their hobbies into businesses at home, often make no impression of seriousness to their clients or customers. Therefore, these businesses are often referred to as "small hobbies", especially if they are not operating full-time. Entrepreneurs are advised to approach their businesses professionally and to relate to business tasks in the same manner, in order to make others take them seriously. On the contrary, their business ideas developed from their hobbies will never develop into a profitable business.

The lack of privacy

Huge professional commitments which need constant engagement, especially if the office is at home, often engage their owners into work past normal working hours. In other words, constant presence in the office influences the lack of privacy and time for rest and other activities. Therefore, it is important to draw a line between professional and private commitments which is only possible if you are managing well your work and free time. Besides that, many people do not know when to stop their work. For example, after dinner an entrepreneur who works at home hurries to his office to finish some work, instead of resting.

The lack of self – discipline

The productivity of workers who work at their homes may vary depending on their level of self-discipline. This means bad time management, which consequently reflects negatively on achieving set goals.

Insufficient attention to marketing

The importance of competition strategy is not seriously taken into account. Actually, many small home business owners think that it is not necessary to pay special attention to public opinion queries in order to determine customers' perceptions of their businesses compared to the competitions'. The problems may arise due to the lack of marketing information, therefore a periodical market analysis is recommended. This analysis should provide the company with the information necessary for their target market.

Human resources management problems

These problems also lead to business failure. This is usually a result of having insufficiently educated and qualified personnel for doing jobs or insufficiently prepared for all economic activities that are expected of them. Family members are often employed in home businesses and this can have consequences for business success. Family members do not necessarily posses the required skills for the job. They often lack expertise and necessary work experience. Therefore, they are an additional fixed expense for the business owner.

Managerial problems

This type of problem is second by importance where business failures are in question. In this domain, problems arise usually from these reasons:

Starting a small business – means the existence of a desire to own a business as well as owning appropriate knowledge and practical skills. Unfortunately, many new business owners underestimate the importance of entrepreneurial knowledge and skills. Without previous experience, education or training, a new owner is weakly prepared to manage and run his new business. The logical solution for gaining practical knowledge is that the new owner was previously employed at someone else's, who ran a similar business.

Business expansion – demands engagement of external expert people, for which a number of new owners aren't prepared at all, because they think that they can handle all work and to control everything on their own. Actually, in business practice, it was considered for a long time that small businesses shouldn't pay much attention to managers and management, which still reflects on many businesses, especially on those which are run from home. In other words, general opinion was that, management was eminent only in large companies. Despite that, in time it became clear that small businesses demand more sophisticated and more organized management than larger companies. Also, the manager role wasn't clear in managing and conducting small businesses.

Thus in some studies, managers are observed from an aspect of their personal qualities, knowledge and capabilities, while in other studies special attention is given to their business results. Also, all types of managers are observed – production managers, sales managers, tourism, marketing, finances, project managers, and their contribution to every business success is evaluated. Lately, project managers became more important, who with their specific knowledge and skills should contribute to make estimation, analysis and evaluation of a project easier, and to help to make certain corrections or complete goal changes in the project on the run if they become inappropriate. Thus the risk is reduced and the possibility of making big mistakes is eliminated, which consequently reduces costs, influences on a higher level of resources use and optimization of time use. One should have in mind that they, with the help of Microsoft Project 2003 tool, as one of the best software of its kind around, must not only measure the results and not only evaluate activities; it is necessary to make a list of project priorities and to hierarchically set tasks and goals in order to follow up on activities and to control effects on the project. Also, in order to paint a realistic picture of a project, it is necessary to review relevant financial indexes. This is of extreme importance because of the relevant valorisation of financial and project investment profitability. This includes the determination of all useful information for making valid decisions related to financial position and the success of a project.

In order to achieve all these, it is necessary to train a manager. The training process should provide appropriate instruments and techniques for every management level. Every one of them should learn organizational processes for project management. One of the best ways to conduct this is by providing project managers with appropriate instructions (manuals) which describe in detail how project managers are supposed to work.

After training, every management level is included into the business with a new set of knowledge and skills for practical work on the project. Education should include not only project managers, but also all employees, so everyone should gain enough knowledge necessary for the job. It is then rightfully expected that all team members will have appropriate knowledge and skills.

Financial problems

Problems in this field appear either because of the inability to provide long-term financial means or because of unexpectedly high financial expenses. Therefore, it is recommended new business owners make a financial plan, in order to avoid those problems.

Lack of planning or Poor Planning

This may lead to making decisions on a daily basis, which reduces the ability of using all available resources. Long-term planning enables the company to anticipate better and to prepare better for the future. However, long-term planning for the majority of small businesses is inadequate, unclear and uncontrolled. According to scientists Peterson and Lille, the key to success for small businesses is the development of managerial expertise. They point out that the critical thing for small companies is not to make a business plan which consists of financial, managerial and marketing components. The reason for this is the fact that most owners lack the knowledge, capabilities or desire to make a business plan. The development plan is also problematic. Unplanned growth may transform successful business activities into their opposites. In other words, if not planned and anticipated, development and growth of a business makes a company unprepared – both financially and managerially.

Isolation from outer world

Working all day at home without contact with the outside world is very stressful, which reflects very negatively in psychological terms on those who own a home business. Therefore, an ability to fight isolation is very significant for those who decide for this way of running a business. Actually, there are a huge number of those who cannot get used to working at home for twelve or more hours without leaving the office and contacts with the outside world. Therefore, they are considered *"prisoners and slaves of their business"*. If you take into account the fact that most of the women run home businesses without any help, then you may find full understanding and an excuse for them saying this type of business is exhausting. Besides that, it is not enough that only women owners adapt to this way of running a business, but also their families and friends.

In order to overcome the mentioned and similar problems, women who work at home are advised: - To occasionally part from their daily activities for one or two weeks. That time should be used for observing all business commitments from a distance, in order to determine whether and in what amount they do some work which unnecessary draws their attention and drains their energy. In this way, they can eliminate idle time, thus reducing their commitments, but also working time. Some psychologists advise organizing meetings with business partners, customers or other associates once a week. In that way, not only is communication expanded, but also the exchange of ideas, information and other things which contribute to the business.

Hiring associates who will be engaged full-time or part-time is also recommended. However, at the same time as engaging with associates and employment of other people, it is necessary to make a calculation of their salaries and fees, because they are a part of overall monthly expenses, which mustn't be neglected.

Practical advice from home business owners to future entrepreneurs

Here we are going to list some advices from experienced entrepreneurs who have long established home businesses and want to share their experiences with those who intend to start their own business. We have selected those, which in our opinion are the most important ones:

1. Be sure that you want to quit your job and become your own boss.

2. Don't do less than your business requires.

3. Surround yourself with people who will provide you with support.

4. Advertise as much as possible and as frequently as possible.

5. Don't be discouraged if you don't have much success at the beginning. Believe in your idea and work hard.

6. Be flexible in your way of thinking, that is, adapt your concept of work to circumstances. In other words, be prepared to change your way of work, the services you offer and the type of product you sell, in order to satisfy your customers' demands.

7. Acknowledge your mistakes and correct them.

8. Develop good contacts with your investors and business partners. Your business survival depends on your cooperation with them.

9. Be well trained for the business, in order to keep business records, use a computer, etc.

10. Avoid complete isolation. Connect to other entrepreneurs who work at home in order to exchange ideas, business experiences and other.

11. Separate your business from your private life. Make a schedule of your daily tasks and jobs. When you are not available to your clients, leave a message on your answering machine, in order to let them know that you will get back to them.

12. Dedicate time for thinking about your business every day. If you are overloaded with commitments, you won't have time to think about the business and to determine in what direction is it moving and what is to be

done next. Under those circumstances, your business will never progress.

13. Dedicate time during every week (three times a week is a recommendation) for some of your hobbies in order to charge your batteries for work that is required of you and other parts of the business.

14. Write down a business plan or let an expert do that for you and update it every year in order to have a clear picture of what you do and where your business is moving towards.

15. Quickly solve your problems and do not let them accumulate.

16. Respond to e-mails instantaneously and be in constant contact with your clients, customers and others.

17. Automatically confirm orders through e-mail.

18. When you meet a like-minded person in business, engage him at once. You need a constant influx of new ideas and creative people.

19. Do not hesitate to ask experts for advice and to ask them for help.

20. Never enter a business without having knowledge about it.

21. Always focus on a single assignment and be fully engaged on its realization.

22. Try to make everything you do as professional as possible. This is the best recommendation for success and high respect from your customers or other users of

your services. If you are not prepared for that, you should not start your business at all.

23. Use the internet. Create your web site, start an electronic magazine as a sort of brochure about your business, buy an advertising banner, join those who are in a similar type of business, etc.

Chapter 6

SETTING AN OFFICE AT HOME

How and under what circumstances should the home office be established?

It is enough to provide one room corner for business and organize it well

When the decision has been made to start a home business, the next step that follows is to establish the home office. There is no specific way of achieving this. Everyone should do it in his/her own way, according to personal preferences. This means that personal desires should be taken into account as well as the work requirements. Having that in mind, some rules should be followed during the home office set-up:

i. Work style

ii. Available space

iii. Necessary equipment for office furnishings

iv. Consider Financing matters

Apart from the above-mentioned conditions which must be taken into account, it is also necessary to consider other rules in order to form work space that would satisfy the business and health criterion of the owner, and his employees, if any. However, it is not always easy to achieve this, as it may seem at first sight. There are usually cardinal mistakes made which may have far-reaching consequences. Some of these mistakes include:

1. Ergonomic conditions not considered

Work space is usually designed according to the financing available, where health implications for employees spending more time there are not considered. Therefore, it is recommended that a risk assessment is carried out to ascertain the likelihood of an injury or other danger, which may put the employee's health at risk. For instance, someone may prefer working at a dining table which maybe of incorrect height or with low illumination in the room, which may both have negative health implications. Sitting on an inappropriate chair may also have negative implications on one's health resulting in back pain neck pain, headaches, etc. The existing household furniture found in the room required for office use is often inappropriate. Instead of existing furniture, it is necessary to choose functional furniture which are appropriate for the type and nature of work to be performed, this will help to reduce discomfort and fatigue. It is most important to invest in a suitable work desk with suitable desk room for the computer and computer accessories without having to constantly stretch, twist and turn to reach items that you need. The chair is the most important piece of the furniture in your office and should be adjustable to different heights so that elbows are roughly the same height with as the key board if using a computer and the backrest adjustable to support the lower of the back to maintain the right posture. Room illumination may also require the appropriate attention, to make sure the room is comfortable to read and does not strain vision. At times it may be necessary to even hiring an interior designer, to design the optimal work equipment and illumination set-up.

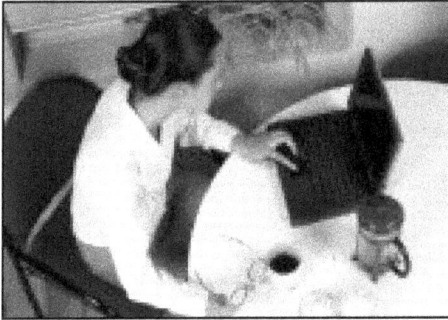

The dining table could never replace the work table – a fact that many neglect in home businesses

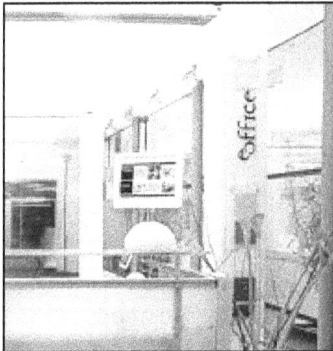

For the ones that could afford it, the special part of the house, with special entrance is highly recommended for the home office establishing

Several hours of work in front of the computer screen may cause some problems which can be manifested in several ways. These can be recognized as eye discomfort, lights spots while looking at far objects, severe headaches, tension and back pains (especially in the neck and shoulder region). The World Health Organization has characterized this type of fatigue as striking mostly eyesight and hearing- the *"video syndrome"*.

Therefore, they recommend numerous advices on how to use the computer, while avoiding such consequences:

- Make short breaks every two hours;

- The monitor position must be checked and the care of the illumination above it;

- Light must be natural, not neon;

- One must not sit in front of the computer screen more than four hours continuously;

- While working on the computer, it is recommended that one looks away from the monitor from time to time, looking away, not focussing on a specific object;

- Occasionally, short exercises for neck and back muscles are recommended.

Having in mind the previously stated facts, it is useful to apply the ergonomic standards while establishing a *home office*, in order to preserve health, provide work safety and achieve higher work productivity.

2. Setting-up the home office in the wrong place

Another mistake which is usually made, is setting-up the home office in the wrong place. For instance, the room might be sound-insulated or near the front entrance, but there is not enough illumination or the area is inadequate (i.e. it is too small) or it is a through room into another area. When the office room is being chosen, the office space must be pleasant, spacious enough with enough day-light and that the person working there must like the room. It is also important to point out that the home office must look like any other office space in a company, outside the house.

Finally, before the final decision is made about the kind of office needed, some other important questions must be answered:

- Do you have everything in one place?

- Do you have enough space for the conference desk?

- Do you have satisfactory technical facilities for the cable internet installing?

Consider these questions with as many details? as possible and try to give answers in writing. They could serve as the checklist to what has been done and what is left to do in your appropriate workspace planning.

Chapter 7

APPEARANCE AND PROFESSIONALISM

How should businesswomen appear when running a business from home?

The attitude towards the work can substantially be expressed through the clothing style one chooses to wear. "...What you wear sometimes shows other people what you think of yourself and your work, and even what you expect from life". Despite that, many people who want to work from home feel that, in this case, clothing does not require significant attention. Accordingly, they perceive informal clothing as a special advantage of working at home. However, this should not go to the extreme, which is, one should not be dressed and act as though performing other house work. That is especially significant in cases where the everyday contact exists with the customers, business partners or other employees. As a matter of fact, inadequately dressed women (in slippers or house gown etc.) will not leave a good impression, nor will she be taken seriously in her business needs and intentions.

"Based on the amount of care given to personal appearance, one could get an impression at first sight that a woman really wants to achieve a successful career". Neglect in clothing usually depicts the neglect in doing business, which can form the impression of distrust and non-professionalism at the very beginning. For instance, if you want to ask for advice from the interior decoration agency, and you are greeted by an untidy, tasteless and inappropriately-dressed business owner or woman manager, you will certainly decide not to hire her for your home or business interior decoration. You will think that if she was not able to make herself presentable and to make a good visual impression, she would most certainly act the same regarding professional business services. In order to avoid this, women are strongly advised to establish respect towards their work, regardless where they perform it – in their house or outside. That way, they will show respect to their clients and partners. "When you dress-up for work, it is necessary to show your intelligence first, and then your femininity." (Klensch, 1996).

This means that more emphasis should be on the face and manners, and less on some physical or female attributes. In other words, in everyday work performing, women must keep their usual dressing style, which should be adjusted to the work type. If a woman does not have the experience of this kind, or she simply does not have a clear picture of how she should usually present herself, it is recommended she take as examples some other businesswomen that have established their own recognizable clothing style, or to consult the literature or experts about appropriate dress.

> "When the woman presents certain gifts and creativity through the clothing she wears, it seems as if she really has something to offer, so she invokes interest and gains greater trust" (Elsa Klensch, 1996).

In this manner, the woman doing business is not only leaving the wanted impression with the business partners and associates, but also increases her self-esteem and feels much more satisfied. At the same time, through the special clothing choice and creating the personal clothing style, she will give special significance to her work and distinguish it from other house chores, just as it should be done regarding the time and work space organizing.

Due to the afore-mentioned, the fact that a home business must not combine with performing other house chores must be stressed again, instead, these should be clearly and precisely distinguished, specified and planned. Similar advice can be translated to men choosing a home business. The thing in common for both of them is that they should be governed by the same rules in clothing choice for performing their business activities:

a) If they own a business in their profession, such as a doctor, dentist, lawyer, business consultant, accountant, professor, etc, it is necessary that their clothing is appropriate for their profession. That is important, because their clients expect professionals to look the part no matter where the job is performed.

b) If they perform a service-oriented business, such as hairdresser, beautician, tailor, among others, the work clothes must also be functional with regard to the job they perform.

c) The persons doing business based on the blue collar work such as car mechanics, home maintenance, locksmith, gardener and similar, must choose the comfortable clothing, which is easy to maintain. It is recommended you wear a uniform or clothing with a company logo. That is the cheapest way to acquire credibility in the client's eyes.

Some basic advice for every businesswoman who wants to appear presentable

According to clothing culture experts' opinion, it is necessary to follow the following advice for business clothing:

- Wear classic, refined, effective and elegant details
- Wear jewellery that frames the face
- Wear high heels, medium to high, which will enable you to look most men straight in the eyes
- Apply make-up well and always use make-up which gives a natural look
- Always wear modern and elegant hairstyles.

The most important advice is that the clothing selection must be in direct correlation with the type of job performed and the frequency of contacts with customers and business associates. Namely, if it is the business where contact with customers and other service users are not necessary, such as music composing, e-business, art and others, somewhat more casual clothing is permissible (jeans, sweaters etc). However, if contact with clients, users, associates and business partners are regular, the clothing style of the entrepreneur can significantly influence the opinion of the business owner and the work he does. Conclusively, if one wants the business to advance, the owner must be dressed to fulfil the customers' expectations and to gain their trust.

Should one work full-time or part-time?

Many entrepreneurs start their home business part-time, due to family commitments and raising children. Others cannot be engaged for more than several hours per day, since their home business is an additional or second job, that is, they have other work obligations. Entrepreneurs usually decide to work from home on a full-time basis when family and financial conditions allow them to do so. This way, they have maximum dedication to their home business, paying their full attention to it, as well as their time, knowledge and money. However, there are many of those who do not pay any attention to making such a decision, since they do not consider it important. Instead, they expect that they will decide in time, after business inception and depending on the scope of activities how much time they would dedicate to the home-business activities performed every day, so they can chose between two options in time – work full or part-time?

When making such a decision, one should realistically consider the existing family situation, finances and spare time which allows the entrepreneur to be dedicated to the new enterprise.

Advantages of Working Part-time

Part-time employment is much less risky than full-time employment and full dedication to one job, which is of special importance for new entrepreneurs without this kind of work experience. Besides that, among the lead advantages of part-time work for home businesses are:

- Providing an extra income;
- Enabling the business to gradually develop and expand, according to the demand for products or services;
- Enabling easier transition from part-time to full-time employment for the business over time;
- Providing full control of different business aspects, such as marketing, sales, promotion, and others.
- Easier balancing of private and professional life;
- Less initial investment for doing business;

- Less pressure for the entrepreneur to make larger profit in the shortest time possible;

- Working part-time at home, the entrepreneur can open numerous possibilities for himself for different personal activities, without the need to sacrifice anything.

Disadvantages of Working Part-time

Even though part-time employment in the home business can present many advantages, it also has numerous disadvantages and negative properties. These include:

- Slow business growth;

- Work professionalism is sometimes questioned as the part-time employed business owners are not seriously perceived by the purveyors, buyers, potential investors and other associates;

- An inability to easily maintain the part-time employment status. As the volume of work grows and the business expands, a greater degree of the entrepreneur's involvement is expected.

Full-time self-employment

It is very hard to make a clear distinction when the part-time employment becomes the full-time one, having in mind that most of the home-business owners spend most of their spare and work time thinking about their business – about marketing strategies, planning and similar issues. Therefore it usually happens that the entrepreneur seamlessly goes over that boundary, and starts dedicating to it full-time, instead of previously part-time engagement.

Even though it is the fact that part-time engagement gives more work liberty and provides many personal choice options, the practice in numerous world-wide countries has shown (here, the USA and other countries with a long tradition of doing business from home are considered) that engagement of this kind is short-lived, and it rather grows fast to full-time employment. It shows certain advantages, which can be illustrated in the following context:

- Full dedication to the work provides easier and faster business idea development;
- Higher degree of professionalism in business;
- Faster development and business progress;
- Business market share increase.

Despite the advantages, some weaknesses can also be stated for full-time engagement. Among the main weaknesses are:

- Greater risk
- Higher initial costs
- Loss of additional job

The aforementioned disadvantages did not significantly contribute to home-business owners discouraging and giving up full dedication to their work. Many of them hold on to the well-known business proverb, *"no great risk in business – no great gain"*.

However, in order to make the right decision regarding the level of commitment to the business, it is very important to consider the business goals set, financing available, and, as mentioned before, family circumstances.

Chapter 8

THE FUTURE OF HOME BUSINESSES

New market expansion possibilities for small home-businesses

It is expected that in some fifteen years, the first wave of the after-war "baby boom" generation will be retiring, which would reflect on the significant growth of senior citizens. Only in the USA that increase estimated to be 17 %, that is, the number of persons older than 65 years shall increase from 33.5 million in the year 1995 to 39.4 million in the year 2010. That trend shall continue between the years 2030 and 2050. By the end of the year 2050, the number of persons older than 65 years in the USA will amount to 79 million. Considering that the population aging trend is also present in our country (we are already considered to be an old nation, due to the negative natural population growth in Serbia), one could rightfully ask the question in this moment regarding the market use of the increase in this market segment, which will have a great share in the total market demand. That is, how is this growth going to change the business environment?

Since people are getting older, they will have different spending and saving models in different phases of their lives. Senior people's needs are significantly different from middle-aged or young people's needs. In view of this, senior citizens have less savings needs than the younger ones, which reflect the increase in their spending. Due to this fact, even now the significant changes regarding the business investments are noted around the world, closely related to changes in the senior citizens tastes. Business chance can be found here for the entrepreneurs performing their work at home for the senior citizens, such as healthcare services provision, food preparation and distribution to old and ill persons, different information and advices provision, preparation of different cultural and other programs etc.

Alternative possibilities for working from home

Doing activities at home has become very popular in the past few years and there appears to be more and more women who opt for this type of self-employment, a huge interest appeared among numerous companies for hiring employees who will do activities needed for the company's business from their homes. Actually, a huge number of companies in the USA and other developed countries in the world learnt that it is much more profitable to hire people to work from home and to make contracts for cooperation with them. According to those contracts, employees are bound to work for their own sake and for the needs of the company which hires them. In this way, during 2000 in the USA 1.2 million people worked, spending in average 35 hours a week in their homes. Compared to 1999, it's an increase of 30 % which indicates a sudden and huge increase of employment of this kind. Experts explain this fact with the companies understanding that it is simpler to hire people who will work from home, than to invest in new equipment, space and to employ a great number of workers, who will create high expenses. Therefore, this type of employment has become especially favoured in large distributing and production companies around the world and expanded in the latter part of the 20th century. Accordingly, many agencies have been founded, which have a huge database with the data about all companies which seek employees in this way (Home Employment Directory).

Having in mind numerous privileges of doing business activity in this way, campaigns have been initiated in many countries, which are conducted under slogan:

"You can become a part of a large family of independent women and men around the country, which are determined to take their fate in their own hands and become their own bosses".

Salaries for this type of work vary from a few hundreds of dollars per week for part time engagement to several thousand dollars for full-time employment. It depends on how much an individual is interested in engaging in order to fulfil his/her personal, professional and other goals. Actually, people are limited only by their desire to succeed and by personal motivation. The only thing that a company asks their employees for is to follow company's simple instructions for work and to regularly and by defined dynamics do their work. In many cases, no special equipment or knowledge is required.

This type of work is very convenient for those women who do not own personal capital, but who would need to invest in doing work from home, as well as to those women who are not willing to completely take the risk of setting up their own business, do not have clearly defined business ideas or sufficient knowledge for running a business individually. Despite the fact that they are not able to manage and run their own private businesses from home, external companies which engage them to work from their homes also provide them with independence in work and the possibility to adjust their working hours to some other commitments (family and other). This type of employment is especially important for single mothers, who don't have any or sufficient financial means for raising their children. Very often, they lack any work experience and some of them didn't work for several years after their child was born so they need to be trained for the job. In such cases, a mentor is assigned to them by their employer, who should provide basic knowledge and skills for these women and to introduce them to work that they should do from their homes. Many companies use a combination of mentor work and video tapes, while other companies decide only for one of those two possibilities.

We will show an example of a woman business owner who engaged 30 other women into her activity, whose task was to do their work from their homes. She was very successful in the coordination of their tasks and activities because she acknowledged their differences regarding knowledge, working experience, talent and efficiency. She adapted training programs for each one of them. Apart from that, she wanted to hear the opinions of all those women and to include their ideas in innovating and improving of her business. Therefore, to every woman, she separately paid 50 USD to think and write down a suggestion for an idea, as well as their vision of business which those women would like to own. Soon she got over 1000 different ideas, 30 of which she instantaneously used and incorporated in her business. It reflected very positively on the business as a whole, which was later explained by the owner as a good treatment of her employees.

Therefore, as that business owner achieved improvements in her business, her other employees achieved many benefits in their jobs and incorporated some of their own ideas, desires and plans in it, thus indirectly influencing business modification and improvement.

Besides previous benefits, this type of engagement of women shows some other qualities. Consequently, in this way, employees can save money and the time they need for every day trips to and from the work place which can be a significant distance from their home. Besides that, they are given the possibility to earn enough money for a supplement to their budget or as a main income source, depending on their level of engagement and success at work. For all those reasons mentioned, this type of employment is becoming very attractive, not only for many companies, but also for women who find an interest in it and can achieve their goals.

Chapter 9

SETTING UP A BUSINESS VENTURE: KEY DECISIONS

Did you choose the right business?

Re-evaluating your personal goals

Project or business plan evaluation is an important part of your journey to setting up a successful business. From the previous chapters, it is recommended that when the feasibility study is finished, it should be checked once again to evaluate whether the choice of business suits the market, as well as the interest and desires of the future business owner - to what extent personal and market interests overlap? At this stage, the most important thing in this phase is to balance personal goals and desires with market demands – did I make the right decision?

In order to illustrate what it looks like when a personal goal harmonizes with the current market demands, we will revisit our practical example:

In the previous case study, we have learned that when Susan worked as an agent for a tourist agency for a number of years she developed interests in setting up her own tourist agency. *Did she set her personal goals from the start?* This was just an untested idea and she did not know what to expect once the business was in motion. After a number of failed attempts she had to re-evaluate her goals – this is an important step we wish to highlight. This is an important stage of a business – buy a new mirror and take another look at yourself! Sue re-assessed her situation whether self-employment was something she needed at that stage of her life or not. She had an option (staying with her current employers).

The desire to achieve your personal goals should be backed by a thorough research into what the current market needs are.

After she organized the first tour through some exotic places of Latin America, Susan published a text in which she pointed out that strong will, persistence, but also consultations with experts helped her in realizing her ambition. Besides that, she advised all those who wish to start similar businesses to ask for advice from specialized agencies which can provide support, help and give an adequate answer to all questions. Not all advices are right – they all have to be tested and matched with the real or current situation.

The advantages of re-evaluating your personal goals

Initially, we had suggested that founding and starting a business can, and usually do influence other aspects of the life of their owners, it is necessary to foresee whether its owner will be able to accomplish some other goals in life besides business i.e. raising a family. This is true as most people tend to either give up on family life to fulfil their business ambitions or isolate themselves from a social sphere. Not having a family could make your business life easier for a short while but the family support is crucial in the long-term. This is could put a lot of strain on a business owner as one part of support disappears. This makes it necessary for one to re-evaluate their personal goals. In doing so, one can accomplish the following benefits:

- Better organization of personal life and work – striking a better balance between personal life and work, learning from initial experience

- Giving oneself alternative options and a best way forward in life – some avenues are not worth following; one becomes able to now focus on the best options.

- Making better and more rational decisions – learning from initial mistakes.

- Higher degree of motivation – at this stage one should know what motivates you most i.e. achievements, money, and status.

- Understand your SWOT – strengths, Weaknesses, Opportunities and Threats – What makes you tick?

- Focusing – one can direct efforts and resources into areas where your strengths are.

As indicated earlier the benefits of personal goals setting are obvious and a large number of women entrepreneurs do not define their personal goals. Activity 4 shows how these goals can be re-evaluated.

Figure 9.4:   *Activity 4* – **Evaluating Your Personal Goals**

Try to answer as objectively as you can the following fifteen questions:

Was having your own business a sole decision you had?

    a) yes   b) no

Did you know your personal and business goals before setting your business?

    a) yes   b) no

Did your personal goals help towards the direction of your business today?

    a) yes   b) no

Was it easy to follow your goals?

    a) yes   b) no

Did your personal goals help you in setting business goals?

    a) yes   b) no

Did you put aside other plans and commitments as a result of your personal goals?

    a) yes   b) no

If you failed to meet some of the goals, did you do anything to adjust the situation?

    a) yes   b) no

Did you assess how your goals have affected your standard of living?

    a) yes   b) no

Was your family life affected?

    a) yes   b) no

Do you accept criticism and admit your own mistakes?

    a) yes   b) no

Are you focused?

    a) yes   b) no

Did you check if there are external factors that might shift your goals?

    a) yes   b) no

Have your goals been translated into business success and financial profit?

    a) yes   b) no

If you have failed completely, are you in a position to look for partners and support from other institutions?

    a) yes   b) no

Where do you see your business in the next 5 years, any new goals?

    a) yes   b) no

It is compulsory to see time as an important factor in running every business and also as an important factor of success. Actually, it is necessary to estimate how much time you need in order to run your own business and then to double that time. Many experts advise those who wish to have a free weekend to "forget" about retail, real estate and service providing businesses. Alternatively, there are other activities that are more flexible and do not need that level of engagement, thus being more easily fitted into one's personal life style.

Determination of educational level and the degree of entrepreneurial skills

When you complete the test we have recommended for determining your inclination for entrepreneurial activities, you will have a partial picture of it. In order to get a complete picture, it is necessary to first determine your general personal knowledge and education, then expert knowledge or various specializations in certain areas and lastly to identify which entrepreneurial skills you have. In total, all this is necessary in order, (apart from provided financial means, location, equipment, partners and business associates, market and other) to make a final decision for starting a business. Many scientists think that knowledge is probably the most important requirement for business success and therefore it is the factor to which the most attention is being paid. Recent research in the USA show that business owners who were not educated enough for the business in which they were engaged were not successful (80 % of their businesses failed during the first year of its existence). On the opposite, those entrepreneurs who were educated and who showed constant interest for improvement have increased their business success (60 %) after the completion of basic training programs for entrepreneurship and management.

One of those scientists who points out the importance of knowledge for business success is the author of the book "Intellectual Capital: The New Wealth of Organization" – Thomas Stewart, who accents intellectual capital as a main determinant of many world companies' wealth. It is important to say that Steward makes a clear distinction between three types of capital – intellectual capital (human), structural and relational capital. Among human capital, he puts individuals with high level education and high intellectual potentials; structural capital consists of patents, various inventions, databases, etc., while relational capital means good contacts with suppliers and customers. When intellectual capital is broken down like this and when a potential entrepreneur makes an introspection of his or her own capabilities and knowledge, then to this should be added the determination of personal entrepreneurial skills, which usually means capabilities for adapting to market demands, self-confidence and certainty in one's own decisions and similar. By this identification and by recognition of your own intellectual and other potentials for doing entrepreneurial and managerial activities, it is not difficult to anticipate what can be expected from future business and to determine one's place on the road to success.

Besides the factors listed above, our intention is to turn attention to potential business owners who are already at the beginning and express certain affinities and prerequisites for founding and running their own company, that, although they rightfully expect success, it does not have to be 100 % guaranteed. To succeed in business, it is necessary to satisfy many other requirements, but also to eliminate many common mistakes at the start. In addition, it is very important to carefully choose business ideas and to determine whether it fulfils all the criteria in your case in order to be transformed to a result-giving business. Accordingly, advice from many scientists and business people state that one should "bet" on good ideas, because only they can bring profit. However, with this statement, we must not forget that ideas cannot be realized in practice without the leadership abilities of women entrepreneurs.

Checking your own knowledge and experiences

In order to check the degree of gained knowledge and practical experience, we can use the concepts developed by Professor Thomas Stewart on classification of intellectual capital in three significant categories; these were discussed earlier in a previous chapter. This classification of intellectual capital can be helpful in determining whether a person has the partial or complete knowledge necessary for the type of business in which that person wants to be successful. In our opinion, this knowledge should be specified and tested by various fields:

General Tests

Figure 9.5: *Activity 5*: **Test on Finances**

Is break-even analysis a technique that you have used before?
    a) yes   b) no
Do you know how to make a financial plan?
    a) yes   b) no
Do you know how to use financial software?
    a) yes   b) no
Do you know when leasing and factoring is used?
    a) yes   b) no
Do you know what your long-term capital sources are?
    a) yes   b) no
Do you have experience in making business plans?
    a) yes   b) no
Do you have experience in presenting business plans to financiers?
    a) yes   b) no

Figure 9.6: *Activity 6*: **Testing your Marketing knowledge**

Do you know different ways to determine the price of a product and service?
    a) yes   b) no
Do you know how to analyze markets?
    a) yes   b) no
Do you have experience with product distribution?
    a) yes   b) no
Do you have experience with product advertising?
    a) yes   b) no
Do you know how to create a marketing plan?
    a) yes   b) no
Do you know how to create an advertising plan?
    a) yes   b) no

Figure 9.7: *Activity 7:* Testing Your General Management Skills

Are you familiar with Employment Law?
   a) yes   b) no
Do you know how to make teams and how to manage them?
   a) yes   b) no
Do you have experience with employees training for new jobs?
   a) yes   b) no
Do you know how to choose the right personnel?
   a) yes   b) no
Do you know how to determine goals and to set work tasks for employees?
   a) yes   b) no
Do you have any experience in relation to idea exchange and information exchange with employees?
   a) yes   b) no
Do you have any experience and knowledge related to employees' needs and their satisfaction, that is, do you know how to motivate employees to be more productive?
   a) yes   b) no

Once you determine your own knowledge and skills and estimate how much experience for the business you have, you will have some ideas and a clearer picture about what areas you should be working on - what direction you should engage in order to fill in the gaps in knowledge and experience. It is interesting to note that many women entrepreneurs think that they do not need managerial experience since most of them prefer micro businesses, which do not demand complex organizational management. However, many experts defend the opinion that due to the lack of knowledge about organizational management their businesses remain small and do not expand (Ronstadt, 1984). In other words, for a company to grow and advance at a faster pace both knowledge and experience are necessary, that is, they must not be overlooked. This is confirmed by the latest research which proves that knowledge combined with experience is a winning combination for team selection and business control.

Training for increasing entrepreneurial knowledge

Training is often considered for new employees only. This is a mistake because ongoing training for current employees helps them adjust to rapidly changing job requirements.

Research has shown specific benefits that a small business receives from training and developing its workers which include:

i. Increased productivity.

ii. Reduced employee turnover.

iii. Increased efficiency resulting in financial gains.

iv. Decreased need for supervision.

Training needs can be assessed by analyzing three major human resource areas: the organization as a whole, the job characteristics and the needs of the individuals. This analysis will provide answers to the following questions:

1. *Where is training needed?*

2. *What specifically must an employee learn in order to be more productive?*

3. *Who needs to be trained?*

When the above questions are answered, a final decision is made on how this training will be realized on a practical level.

There are two broad types of training available to small businesses: on-the-job and off-the-job techniques. Individual circumstances and the "who," "what" and "why" of your training program determine which method you use:

On-the-job training is delivered to employees while they perform their regular jobs. In this way, they do not lose time while they are learning. After a plan is developed for what should be taught, employees should be informed of the details. A timetable should be established with periodic evaluations to inform employees about their progress. On-the-job techniques include orientations, job instruction training, apprenticeships, internships and assistantships, job rotation and coaching.

Off-the-job techniques include lectures, special study, films, television conferences or discussions, case studies, role playing, simulation, programmed instruction and laboratory training. Most of these techniques can be used by small businesses although, some may be too costly.

Training programs should be well-designed and should consider the ability of the employee to learn, the materials, and should make the most efficient use of resources. It is also important that employees be motivated by the training experience. Employees' failure in the program is not only damaging to the employee but a waste of money as well. Selecting the right trainees is important to the success of the program.

Chapter 10

COMMUNICATION

Importance of Good Communition Skills for Managers and Entrepreneurs

Communication skills for managers and entrepreneurs are vital ingredients in business ventures. Most managers recognise that communication skills are essential in business. Entrepreneurs or owner-managers need to be able to communicate, build relationships and work with individuals at all levels. Their behaviour and interpersonal skills can affect others both positively and negatively.

Introduction

Communication is an essential part of any company. Moreover, good communication skills are incredibly important in the business world. In an article by Geraldine J. Tucker[1], she discusses the many ways to manage and deal with difficult communication. She attests that the point of communication is having a conversation with another person, and this conversation must be two-way in order for communication to successfully occur. This central idea is important to remember, especially during times of conflict. In fact, *"you are not being effective when your voice rises, your body tenses, or your temper flares," giving in to emotions often prevents successful communication, which often times can damage businesses and business relationships* (Tucker, 2007: 806).

Tucker believes that in order for successful communication to occur two things must be kept in mind; the first is that everyone has their own ideas and their own perceptions and these must be respected and the second is the idea of closure, that every conversation needs closure. Tucker states, you need to keep in mind that each person comes to the table (conversation) with his or her own perception of what happened, what exists, or how to do something. It doesn't help the situation to negate a person's viewpoint without facts and concrete examples of behaviour or acts that were considered inappropriate, unprofessional, or unacceptable. However, it is important to communicate until you get "closure" on the conversation. Closure means you and the other person have discussed all of the issues and, while the person may not agree, he or she has listened to you in a non-threatening, non-defensive environment and clearly heard what you had to say (Tucker, 2007).

This concept is incredibly important to remember in the corporate environment. Companies are made of various types of employees and managers, each with their own personalities and viewpoints. Therefore, it is important to remember to respect everyone's opinions no matter how different they may be. Also, the notion of closure in a conversation is essential because leaving a conversation up in the air or even with hostility can often result in damaging or breaking business relationships. Good communication is necessary in order for businesses to run successfully and smoothly.

Definition of Communication

Communication is the act of sending a message through different media; it can be verbal or nonverbal, formal or nonformal so long as it transmits a thought provoking an idea, gesture, action, etc. Good communication is considered a learned skill. Most people are born with the physical ability to talk, but we must learn to speak well and communicate effectively. Speaking, listening, and our ability to understand verbal and nonverbal meanings are skills we develop in various ways. We learn basic communication skills by observing other people and modelling our behaviours based on what we see.[2]

Nature of Communication

The concept of communication is a vital one for any organisation be it a private company or a public parastatal like Federal Ministry of Education, Ministry of Finance, Universities. For instance, a lot has been said about the importance and usefulness of information to management at all levels in all organizations whether big or small, and irrespective of the nature and orientation or objective of the firm.

It is, however, important here to point out that information is of little use until it is communicated to the person who is to receive it or who has the need for it. Communication, is therefore, a process of transmitting, disseminating or passing information from one person to the other or from one place to the other. In other words, communication is the process of creating, transmitting and interpreting ideas, facts, opinions and feelings. It is a process that is essentially a sharing one, a mutual interchange between two or more persons (Cole 1990)[3]. Using the more technical terms. Communication can be perceived as the process of sending information from an encoder, through a channel to a decoder.

Finally, communication is the exchange of information managers. This exchange is usually to influence decision making behaviour and employee. It is also what enables managers and organizations to achieve high performance. In addition, it is also what enables and employees to co-operate and organise.

The most effective managers are those who understand communication and its use in the organisational setting. Communication is the vehicle that allows managers to fulfil each management function. To plan successfully, managers must be able of effectively communicate their vision to the rest of the organization. To organize successfully, managers must allow for and encourage free-flowing communication both up and down the hierarchy, as well as between departments and colleagues.

To lead successfully, managers must clearly communicate organizational goals to employees and through that communication, inspire employees to trust in their leadership and to perform at the highest levels possible. To control successfully, managers must effectively communicate with employees to monitor progress to re-emphasize organizational goals, and to correct on-going processes. Consequently, communication is more than simply talking, writing, reading and listening. Effective communication is the key to successful management.

Communication allows managers to share goals with shareholders both inside and outside the organisation. It permits managers to stimulate behaviour changes in employees and suppliers. It enable managers to inspire loyalty from employees and customers. It allows managers to convice employees and unions to abandom counter productive practices. It enables managers to persuade leaders to provide financing and it permits managers to calm angry customers and to impress new ones.

Hence, managers must be effective communicators to function. *But what makes managers and entrepreneurs successful communicators?*

First, they must understand what communication is. Next, they must understand how communication works, on both an interpersonal and an organisaional level and finally, they must understand what barriers can impede communication so that they can overcome such impediments and improve communication throught the organization.

In the modern day organizations, communication is popularly considered in terms of; the media of communication such as internal memoranda, reports of various forms, etc; the skills of communication such as giving instructions, interviewing, chairing meetings, etc and the organization of communication like chain of command, briefing groups, work committees, etc. However, communication at its basic levels involves three basic elements or components, which are encoder, channel and decoder. The source or the origin information is known as the encoder. That is, the encoder is the originator of the information to be communicated to the other party. The channel is the medium chosen or to be used in communicating the message or information to other party. The decoder is the person to whom the message or information is being sent. He is the receiver of the message. However, he/she may, or may not, be the user of such an information. For instance, if the Managing Director of company 22 telephoned the personnel manager of copany 33, the managing director is the encoder, the telephone line the channel and the personnel manager is the decoder in this exapmle. However, the three of them must always be present regardless of the size or system of communication. A typical communication model may be as presented follows.

Figure 10.8: *Communication System Model*

Encoder   Information   Decoder

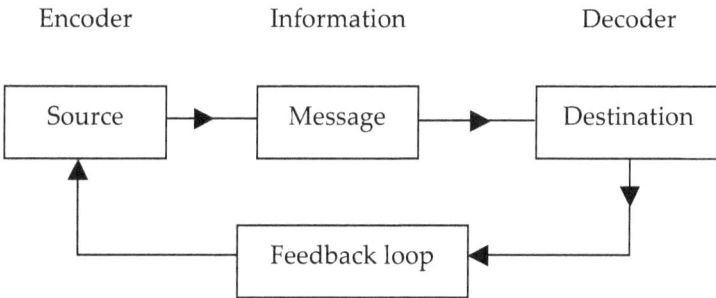

From Fig. 10.8, it can be seen that communication is the process by which the senders and the receivers of information interact in a given social context. Information conveyed might be message, instruction, idea, view or knowledge. It may be communicated from superior officer to a subordinate officer, and vice-versa. It may also be communicated across among colleagues at the same level or having similar status along the organizations hierarchy.

However, communication process in modern organizations normally follows the pattern bellow:

a)   The sender has an idea,

b)   The idea becomes a message. Remember that the process of putting the message into a form the receiver will understand is called encoding,

c)   the message is transmitted to the receiver,

d)   The recever gets the message and interpret it, a process known as decoding, and

e)   The reveicer feedback the sender about the effectiveness of the information that was communicated.

From our discussion so far, we would observe that the process of encoding involves determination of the way that the message should be written down or spoken in order to be able to communicate with another person. Variation of words and understaning can however alter the meaning of a message. Facial expression, voice, emphasis and gestures; all play a part in the encoding process when conversation is used. Also, it is clear that the decoding is the process of achieving understanding from the message. Different people derive different meanings from the same message influenced by their experience, attitudes and value systems.

Forms of Communication

Forms of communication include written, verbal, formal and informal communication. Written communication encompasses letters, memos, notes, emails and all other forms of writing. Verbal communications include face-to-face discussions, phone calls, e-chatting over the Internet and group meetings. Both verbal and non-verbal communication is extremely important with in the business world and also in people's personal lives. Being able to communicate properly can make uneasy situations or tough times much easier to handle, remaining calm and understanding can lead to resolving uncomfortable situations. One of the biggest components of being a good communicator is being a good listener. Without the ability to listen you cannot be a good communicator.

Good communication skills are essential in the business world for three main reasons:

1. Firstly, ineffective communication can be very expensive. If a business does not communicate effectively and efficiently to employees, its objectives, rules and regulations, along with its business culture, then the employees will not be effective in the work place. If employees cannot communicate with each other, regardless if the communication is horizontal or vertical with in the business, things will not run smoothly. Without good communication things may not get done correctly or even at all, or, work could be done twice, overlapping each other, which can be wasteful and costly. Good communication is essential for business operations in all aspects of business.

2. The changing environment and increasing complexity of the 21st century workplace makes communication even more important today, than ever before. The flattening of business structure and the increase in teamwork in the work place demands good communication skills. Flatter organizations mean managers must communicate with many people over whom they may have no formal control. Without communication teamwork is impossible and will fail to provide any useful outcome. The collaboration of teamwork that allows organizations to capitalize on the creative potential of a diverse workforce depends on good communication.

3. The world's economy is becoming increasingly global, meaning people need to be able to communicate not only within the organization but also outside the organization and even at times internationally. To be a good communicator internationally you need to understand who you are trying to communicate with. What is their culture? Can something be offensive to others, which is not offensive to you? It is important to be have proper communication skills and to be aware of others' culture to be an effective communicator.

We don't believe that either a man or a women is superior at communicating, rather we believe that both can be effective communicators as long as they know who and what they trying to communicate. Remaining calm and being a good listener are key to being a good communicator. We think it is possible for both men and women to be great communicators but it doesn't usually come without working at being a good communicator.

When it comes to difficult conversations or having to communicate bad news it is useful to remain calm, be understanding, listen completely, put yourself in the other's position and be clear when communicating. Now there is a lot there to grasp but if you can do those things it will easy the pain when communication become difficult regardless of the circumstances.

Non-verbal communication is important and useful because without saying anything someone can determine what it is you are trying to get across. Non-verbal communication can be misleading if your point is misunderstood, since you are not directly speaking your intentions. But if the message is correctly interpreted non-verbal communication is extremely powerful.

In all, good communication is important in the work place and in our personal lives. Without good communication the message is lost, time is wasted and people can feel betrayed, so becoming both a good listener and good communicator is essential to day-to-day life.

Presentation communication is also an integral part of a company's success. If an employee has a brilliant idea for reducing cost and they have an opportunity to present it to the President they must make the most out of the opportunity. Effective presentation skills require practice, patience and the ability to stay calm in stressful situations. Along with presentation skills comes listening. If someone is giving a presentation it is important that you are able to listen and understand. This will help the company if everyone is able to share the information.

4. Lastly, there is cross-cultural communication. Language barriers and cultural differences can hinder a firm's productivity and efficiency, thus putting the company at a disadvantage. Overcoming these barriers and increasing communication skills will help the company reach its full potential.

Difficult communication

Difficult communication is important to deal with successfully, especially within a company. We can identify many obstacles to effective communication (table 1).

Table 10.1: Obstacles to Effective Communication

Obstacles to Effective Communication
• Assumptions
• Fears
• Reluctance to confront
• Ridicule, rejection, fear of being wrong
• Authority relationships
• Unmanaged stress

Tucker[4] lists seven more objectives of dealing with communication issues. These issues can range from misunderstandings, difference of opinions, and so forth. He believes that it is most important to remain objective when disagreements arise. It is important to put yourself in the other person's shoes in order to understand their viewpoint. Without sympathizing with the person you are conversing with there is more of a possibility of the conversation to become argumentative and defensive. Tucker listed the second most important aspect of dealing with difficult communication; responding to the content and not the person. Often times people make the mistake of "shooting the messenger" rather than addressing what the messenger is saying. Tucker states, "Difficult communication arises when people perceive that their ideas or "selves" are being attacked". Again the notion of being defensive arises once more. Tucker continues on with tips that eventually lead to a resolution of the bad communication. In order for difficult communication to be resolved, one must be aware of all the facts, other people's feelings, and personal restraint.

There is a certain need for control when it comes to successful communication. This control applies to managing of emotions, personal beliefs, and even facial expressions. Emotions aren't always logical and when it comes to business, sometimes emotions tend to get in the way. Emotions such as anger very often can impede the process of a new business plan. Also, clashing of personal beliefs can often lead to arguments and very often personal life should be kept out of the corporate world. Facial expressions tend to be misinterpreted; a slight rolling of the eyes could ruin a potential relationship between client and organizations. Nonverbal communication can be potentially beneficial for an organization; however, the meanings of the nonverbal messages need to be shared, otherwise they risk being misinterpreted and result in miscommunication. For example, a friendly smile can be used as a sense of encouragement or telling someone they did a great job.

Formal Communication Channels

Communication channel simply refers to the medium through which a message or information gets from the origin to the destination. That is, the channel by which the message gets from the sender (or encoder) to the reciever (user or decoder).

In the contemporary private and public organizations, the channels of managemet information include the Newspaper, magazines, radio and television announcements / broadcasting, company journals, employees hand- books, notice boards telephone converstion, telex, telefax, telegram, intercoms, post office or postal services, internet, report, pictures, graphics and cartons, personal contact, libraries, and sending errand boys and messagers. Others include information obtained simply by looking around; letter writing; internal memoranda; statutory books; textbooks etc. All these are common in the modern day business and non-business organizations as a means of communication.

Informal Communication Channels

Apart from the formal medium or channel of communication, contemporary managers and administrators in organisation still have to graple with a number of unofficial or informal channels of communication if they want their operations to progress as planned or according to target. Informal communication is the flow of information without regard for organisational structure, hierarchy level or reporting relationship. All sorts of soft information such as rumours and gossip etc are carried through informal communication.

Informal communication structures have no set direction and they evolve from employee's interpersonal and social interactions. It moves primarily through word of mouth and one common form is the grapevine; an informal channel of person to person communication that is not officially sanctioned by the organisation. Grapevine is usually one of four structures as follows:

a)   *Single Strand Chain:* In the single strand chain, each person passes the information on to one other person. The longer the chain, the more the information is prone to distortion.

b)   *The Gossip Chain:* In this case, information is moved slowly because it depends on one person telling everyone else. The usual structures is as follows:

Figure 10.9: *A Single Strand Chain*

Figure 10.10: *The Gossip Chain*

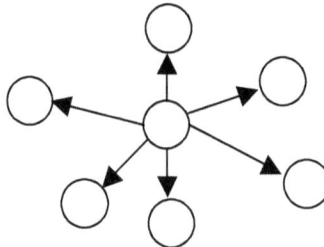

c) *The Probability Chain:* This is the type of information which has no definite pattern of communication. One person passes along information at random and receiver in turn passes it randomly to others – so some people hear the information and others do not. The normal structure of this type of communication is as follows:

Figure 10.11: *The Probability Chain*

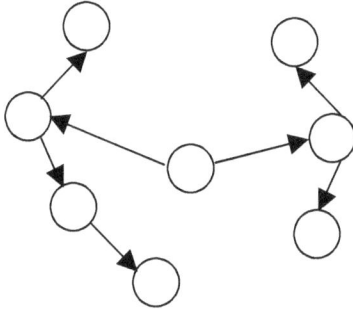

Figure 10.12: *The Cluster Chain*

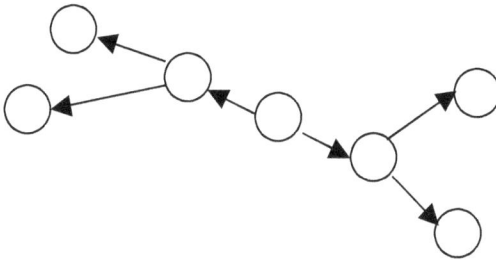

d)   *The Cluster Chain:* This is the most predominat pattern, information is passed along selectively. One employee passes information to co-workers, who passes it along to other co-workers. In this grapevine structure, people relay information to those with whom they feel most comfortable.

When managers and employees don't receive what they consider to be full information from formal channels, they seek it from informal sources. The more the formal communication system witholds relevant information from employees, the more employees seek to develop informal communication networks which can often work against the purposes of the formal organization. However, effort to get rid of the grapevine often makes it more powerful. Grapevine flourishes in climate of high uncertainty, when information from formal channel is especially scarce.

When grapevine passes inaccurate or unconfirmed information, especially rumoured layoffs, employees who cannot verify the truth may feel demoralized. Some organizations have to set up formal communication channels to difuse the anxiety caused by grapevine rumour. Employees consider the grapevine as a highly credible source, so they cannot ignore information that flows through it. Mangers can use it to unofficially propose new ideas and monitor employee reaction to them. The response, however, gives clues to how the proposal could be reversed for better acceptance.

Conclusion

Effectively communication can be a very useful tool when it comes to confrontation. In the work place confrontations occur, that is no surprise. However, effective communication can put many of these issues to bed if used properly. In a stressful situation an effective communicator will be able to "defuse" the situation. This applies not only to aggressive confrontations but also to conflicts of interest. One team member may want to follow option A while another wants to follow option B. The effective communicator will lay out the positives and negatives of both options and gather everyone's opinions on the situation. This not only provides a majority decision but also a calm resolution to a problem. The idea of whether women are better communicators than men is circumstantial. Sure women tend to engage in more and lengthier conversations than men, but this is dependent on personality. There are far too many stereotypes that portray women as talkers and even more persuasive than their male counterparts. However, this is incredibly subjective. Environment and upbringing is the one factor of whether or not someone, despite gender, can become a good communicator. The argument based on the beliefs of society that deems women as more conversational is simply not enough to support the idea that women make better communicators than men. The article by Tucker does not write to a specific gender because communication problems and successes are experienced by both men and women.

Technology has come a long way, and as easy as it is for us to communicate with people, it is just as hard to understand. For example, face to face communication is not as common as it once was, therefore, emails and written forms of communication have become more common. Although easily accessible, it eliminates the non verbal part of communicating such as facial expressions, tone, pitch etc. Although these things seem minor, they are vital to communicating as they relay sincerity, sarcasm, and other qualities of communication. Without this nonverbal form of communication, people are quick to assume and may not always be assuming correctly.

Notes

[1]   Tucker, Geraldine J. "Managing Difficult Communication." *Texas Bar Journal:* Vol. 70, No. 9. p. 806-807., October 2007.

[2]   Mehrabian and Ferris (1967). "Inference of Attitude from Nonverbal Communication in Two Channels". In: *The Journal of Counselling Psychology* Vol.31, 1967, pp. 248-52.

[3]   Cole G. A., (2003), "Management Theory and Practice", High Holborn House, London

[4]   Op. cit., 185 page

Chapter 11

FRANCHISING

Another form of flexible business ownership available for women is franchising. Unlike many new businesses, the entrepreneur enters with a high degree of uncertainty and business risks until the business is fully implemented and successful. In franchising, the entrepreneur starts his business with much less business risk, considering that it is already a developed business, and he or she is just joining in.

Defining Franchising

The franchising is defined as a type of business arrangement where the product (service) producer or distributor gives the exclusive rights to the local distributor to do the sales himself, according to the standardized business procedure. The person offering the goods or service to be franchised is referred to as the franchiser (products or services owner) and provides the license transfer to the franchise buyer in order to distribute its goods, regardless of whether it is wholesale or retail.

Many senior and retired persons are going to increasingly open home offices, which will enable them to earn some extra income, but also to feel business valid and vivid. They will also be able to meet their generations' requirements, since they will be better acquainted with their needs structure.

Franchising can also be defined as the economic instrument for wish-come-true; for acquiring business self-sufficiency with minimal risk and investments and maximal chance for success by use of verified products and services and marketing methods. International Franchising Union defines the franchising as "the continual retail, where the franchiser provides the license for doing business, organizational, training and management assistance with a fee charged from the person taking the goods on franchise."

What is the fee amount and how is it paid?

Franchising is just another possibility for starting a business, but in this case an already developed business idea, company name, company's image, knowledge and experience are being utilized provided by the franchiser for the entrepreneur to use for which he charges a fee. This fee can be paid to the franchiser weekly or monthly, depending on the signed franchising contract and it is usually calculated as the percentage of goods or services turnover, not profit. This percentage is variable, and it could be 2-20 %, depending on the business scope and agreement between the contractual parties.

Franchising history

Franchising is more than 150 years old, but it started to appear in the present form since 50s of the previous century. The most familiar franchising example is the one related to the fast food production, where the most successful example is McDonald's.

In the past few years, franchising continues its growth with regard to the number of employees, diversity of products offered for sale and also represents one of the best options for the entrepreneur to increase his/her competition abilities in comparison with large companies. Due to that fact, in developed capitalistic countries, franchising is used in more than 70 % of production and other service-providing businesses, and more than 50 % of the retail turnover is contributed to it. According to the International Trade Administration data, 478,000 franchises in USA had participated with 576 billion USD in the total turnover for the year 1996. During the year 1999, the study was performed in the USA, showing that in the past five years 86 % of this kind of businesses had been founded, with a further growth trend (source: The United States Chamber of Commerce, 1999). According to the same source, during the period from 1991 to 1997, only 5 % of these kinds of businesses were closed down, which is an extremely important indicator of this business conducting method's stability. This claim is also confirmed by the information that during the previously mentioned period, some 62 % of companies were closed down because the business was conducting errors and such like, which were not organized and managed using the franchising principles. Another fact is that approximately 30 % of franchisers had been earning more than $150,000 per year, during the year 2000.

Having this in mind, one may say that the franchise represents a good, simple and successful solution for many businesspersons. It is an especially important solution for situations where one of the factors contributing to business success is missing (market, labour, financing, equipment etc.) However, in order to use all of the advantages the franchise provides, the entrepreneur must be informed in advance, about what the franchise is, what its advantages are, as well as regarding the potential risk.

Types of Franchising

Several types of franchising exist, although other forms may develop as a result of franchising innovations. One of the most important types of franchising was incepted in the automobile industry. In this case, the producers use the franchise for distribution of their product lines. Many franchises offer services such as real estate trade, agency services, etc. Great possibilities for franchising exist in agriculture and in rural areas, in country tourism and homemade craftwork, processing or preparation of agricultural products for industrial production. These services include well-known names, reputation and business performing methods.

Women and franchising

Women's interest in franchising is not proportional to the possibilities it provides. It is still considered that this is a man's area of business. Therefore, women are very slowly joining this type of doing business. For these reasons, many companies wish to attract as much women as possible wanting to enter franchising, so one can notice large companies around the world dedicated to women as the main target group. Sometimes these companies may be significantly aggressive, because they are trying to attract the attention of as many women as possible at any cost. Some of them manage to do so, especially the ones managed by women, which makes them attractive enough for other women to join the business. Generally, franchising is becoming a more and more significant area of self-employment for both women and men. According to the Nat-West/British Franchise Association data, franchising generates new jobs every year and employs approximately 326,000 people in Great Britain

In the USA, approximately 3.5 % of all businesses owned by women are a franchise. Besides that, according to some researches, regarding the total franchise business structure, more than one third consists of women entrepreneurs. A similar situation can be observed in other highly developed countries. For instance, according to the NatWest/BFA survey from 2003, among the new franchisers in the Great Britain, approximately 26 % were women. That percentage had increased for 10 % compared with several previous years. This type of business is not very common in the developing world.

Bearing in mind that the franchisers are looking for well-trained, qualified and success-oriented women, the question is asked: *what must one know to enter this kind of business, and what are the advantages and disadvantages of running a franchise?*

Risk takeover and franchise investment risk

Successful business expansion by means of franchise requires great understanding of what should be done to develop the franchise system. The franchise grantee should know, besides his/her rights and duties defined in the franchise contract, how fast he/she should develop, how much support he/she needs, how he/she should solve problems, etc.

If the franchiser does not possess enough knowledge in this area or does not know how to transfer it to the franchise buyer, serious problems may occur. Problems usually appear if there is no franchising plan and program due to the insufficient communication between the contracted parties etc. It is also necessary that both parties are acquainted with the details of the franchise expenses (legal expenses, registration expenses, current market expenses, expenses regarding publishing of the brochure used for the sales and the cost of the training material for the franchise grantee). Besides that, the franchise expenses should include the expenses of products (services) commercials, market research expenses, consultants' fees and the enterprise location visits.

Just like any other business, a franchise is not meant for a passive person. It requires business effort that involves many hours of preparation in order to assure that the business will run efficiently. Likewise, each entrepreneur should go through self-testing in order to be sure if the franchise is the right choice for him. Answering the following questions may serve as the directions for the entrepreneur if his decision is right.

- Are you starting on your own?
- Do you enjoy working with other people?
- What makes your business unique or different from others?

- Are you prepared to continue the business initiative even if work is progressing or stagnating?
- Are you of good health?
- Do you have different delivery methods?
- Do you have different marketing strategies?

Prospective entrepreneurs should also know if there is enough demand for their products and services. If the prospective entrepreneur, deciding to franchise can answer most of the questions asked with YES, he/she has a great chance to succeed in his/her dedication.

Advantages of franchising

One of the most important advantages of franchising is the fact that the entrepreneur does not encounter the usual problems of business inception. The franchiser usually provides the plan with clear instructions for conducting the business. That way, the one getting the franchise of the business gets suggestions or even clear definition of its business location. Location analysis provides a level of certainty that the business will achieve desired and defined objectives. The franchise often includes trademark use by the franchise buyer, which provides him/her with instant recognition in the market. That does not assure the business success, but it enables the business to start with a positive image.

Table 11:2   Advantages of buying a franchise

1. Product or service already have a market and a recognizable image;

2. Formula or design are patented;

3. Trademark;

4. High level of business success;

5. A financial management system for financial results control;

6. Managers' advice in this domain;

7. Bulk economy for commercial and purchase;

8. Proofed business concept;

9. Top management services;

10. Financial assistance;

11. Business method development;

12. Territorial protection and market domination;

13. Standardized product or service;

14. Larger market breach than without franchise;

15. Business conducting manual;

16. Long-term market research;

17. Business conducting training;

18. Business inception full support

19. Efficiency-profitability

20. Profit maximization

Regarding the franchising, one can also add that it is successful when both contractual parties are profitable. Without both parties profitability, franchise is unsuccessful. Therefore, one may rightfully claim that franchising is far from a simple business, it can be the launching platform for a small business or long-term good ideas, but it can also lead its founders into difficulties if they do not develop the franchise system well enough.

How can one assure the success of a franchise?

In order to assure franchise success, it is necessary to provide appropriate conditions and to pay attention to several key preconditions, such as:

- Franchiser must always present to the franchise buyer the way to enhance the product or service;

- Franchiser analyses every target market, in order to assure long-term business development and profit in that market;

- Franchiser should understand that the business can develop and open only by providing constant support for the franchise buyer.

Franchising contract items

When drafting the franchising contract, the professional advice by the lawyer with significant experience in this domain is necessary. The contract consists of all specific franchise requirements and obligations. The most important requirements which stand out are license transfer of the franchiser to the franchisee with appropriate protected rights (copyrights, trademarks, know-how and other). These rights are time and space limited. Financial requirements shall be included in the initial franchise price, payment outline and timetable (dynamics), etc.

The contract, produced in written form, should contain the items listed in the Table below.

Table 11.3: Franchising contract elements

Franchiser identification and Business experience

Initial funding to be provided by the franchise buyer;

Franchise grantee is obligated to pay a percentage from goods or services turnover during the contract validity;

Payment continuity;

Franchise grantee training program;

Present franchise grantees number;

Franchise grantee's financial situation;

List of other franchise grantees' names and addresses;

Franchise implementing territorial protection;

Products or services available for franchise grantee work definition;

All financial sources available for the franchise buyer;

Business control performed by the franchise granter (financial control, products or services control, etc.)

Franchise contract duration varies from one to twenty-five years and more. According to the researches performed in the USA, the most usual are contracts for a 10 year period (33.1 %), followed by contracts for 20 years (19.6 %), while the smallest number are one-year contracts (1.1 %).

Choice of the franchising consultant

Before the choice of a consultant is made, the following details should be considered:

1. Which segment of the business requires help – management, marketing, sales or financing?

2. It is necessary to perform the interview with several consulting companies, in order to determine if they

possess the expertise for the domain needing assistance;

3. The inquiry should be made on how the consulting knowledge could be related to the company's specific needs;

4. How much do the consulting services cost?

5. For how long should the consultants be hired?

6. Do the consulting company's employees share the same business opinions, together with the owners?

7. Are the consultants located near the hiring company?

8. Is the consultant proficient regarding not only the franchising, but also regarding the company's production?

Franchise disadvantages

Besides the presented advantages, this method of business activity performing also shows certain disadvantages. Among the most important, the following disadvantages should be noted:

- Liberty limitation when buying a franchise;
- Limited production line;
- Time limitation of the franchise contract;
- Franchise sales limitations.

Besides that, if the contract was not written well, numerous misuses might occur.

Chapter 12

CONCLUSIONS

The previous 11 chapters have highlighted the women in business phenomenon and have provided different flexible approaches that women can opt for when choosing to set up their business ventures. Other chapters have focused on setting business at home – which is the most flexible way of balancing both work and family. Businesses that women do at their homes are relatively new. These are usually smaller businesses in the field of providing intellectual and other services. With the great technology of the Web, many people are choosing to work from home. Not only are some offices allowing their employees to telecommute, but people are also starting their own home businesses with websites or affiliate programs. There are so many opportunities out there and some of them have been mentioned in this book.

According to many indexes, these businesses are very stable, which is affirmed by data that the average age of businesses that women run from their homes is around six years. Also, according to research of "National Foundation of Women Business Owners" (1997), women home business owners much more than other women business owners use credit cards and their own personal means for financing businesses. Women are proving to be resilient when it comes to falling in debt traps as most seem to avoid depending on loans and credits. This does not suggest that women do not need credits, but it is a realisation that women are emerging as business owners despite the difficult conditions.

Despite the different motivational factors, which lie behind the start-up of the new businesses, the common thing for most women entrepreneurs and managers is that with their increased participation in the business world they give a significant contribution and influence management style, giving it a "female mark". Also, women tend to start some new types of businesses. These businesses provide room for employment of other women, who comparatively makeup the largest group of unemployed. In that way, in many countries women in business have become the main power of economic progress and they are rightfully meant to be relied on in the future.

In addition, in this book we have tried to systematically introduce the basic laws of entrepreneurship to students and entrepreneurs by providing them with the necessary bases for individual performance of their future entrepreneurial activities. Their theoretical knowledge on entrepreneurship, supported with practical examples and experiences, can later be used and improved through individual work. At the same time, we would like to mention that skills, once learned, need to be permanently improved, innovated, supplemented and adapted to business demands.

At the end of the day, it can be concluded that a new economy sets new standards of success and opportunities for new start-up ventures which are related to forming strategic alliances, new technology use, experiences and knowledge exchange among entrepreneurs and their counterparts. There is an emerging power of social capital and networking that seem to overcome individuality. This is something that small businesses, and female-owned business in particular, must not ignore.

REFERENCES

Calas, Martha B., and Smircich, Linda, (1996). From 'The Woman's' point of view: feminist approaches to organization studies' in Handbook of organization studies. In S. Clegg, C. Hardy, and W. Nord (eds.), 218-257. London: Sage.

Casson, Mark C. (1982). *The Entrepreneur. An Economic Theory.* Oxford: Martin Robertson

Delmar, F. and P. Davidsson (1998), 'A taxonomy of high-growth firms'. In: P. D. Reynolds et al. (eds.): Frontiers of Entrepreneurship Research http://www.babson.edu/entrep/fer/papers98/XIV/XIV_A/XIV_A.html

G.A. Cole, (2003),"Management Theory and Practice", High Holborn House, London

Hisrich, R.D., and Brush, C.G. (1986), *The Woman Entrepreneur: Starting, Managing and Financing a Successful New Business* (London, Lexington Books).

Klensch, Elsa (1996) "Style", Belgrade

Maika, Valencia (2007). "The past of female entrepreneurship with the stress on the future in the new economy- globalization" in the book (Mirjana Radović Marković editor),"The Perspective of Women`s Entrepreneurship in the Age of Globalization", IAP, Charlotte

Radović Marković M. (1994). "Vodič za uspešan biznis", UMS, Beograd

Radović Marković M. (2006). "Theoretical and Practical Guide for all aspects for Starting up Small Business", Link group, Belgrade

Radović, Marković Mirjana (2006). "Entrepreneurship: Theoretical and Practical guide on all aspects for starting up Small Business", Link group, Belgrade

Radović-Marković, Mirjana (1995). "Supplements on Entrepreneurship in Entrepreneurship, in Economic and Business Encyclopedia", Savremena, Belgrade

Radović-Marković, Mirjana (1996). " Economic Analysis on the New (Quantitative) Basis, Faculty of Economics, Belgrade.

Radović-Marković, Mirjana (2005)."Leaders Abilities of Woman and Their Position in the Business World," Teme, University of Nis, Nis, July-September

Radović-Marković, Mirjana (2006). "Managers and entrepreneurs skills as key contributors to SME success in the future business challenges", *Serbian Journal of Management: an International Journal for Theory and Practice of Management Science,* Bor, University of Belgrade, Technical faculty, Management Department, 2006-, 2007, god. 2, br. 1, pp. 93-99

Radović-Marković, Mirjana (2006)."Woman Entrepreneurship and Leaders Abilities of Women and Their Position in the Business - (case study of Serbia and Balkan region)", International Journal, Vol. 1, Issue 3, Punjab College of Technical Education, India

Radović-Marković, Mirjana (2007). "*Women entrepreneurs and managers in Serbia", Journal EKONOMIKA A MANAZMENT PODNIKU,* roc. 5, 2007, c., page 5-15.

Tucker, Geraldine J. (2007). "Managing Difficult Communication." *Texas Bar Journal:* Vol. 70, No. 9. p. 806-807., October 2007.

INDEX

B

Brainstorming, 19, 35
Bulk economy, 143
business owners, ix, 1, 13, 46, 54, 65, 66, 71, 76, 78, 85, 86, 88, 89, 104, 105, 115, 116, 147

C

Cantillon, Richard, 2
Cluster Chain, 133
Communication, 121, 122, 123, 124, 125, 126, 129, 130, 131, 135, 150
Corporation, 55, 56, 57

D

Dallas, 45
Documentation review, 72

E

entrepreneurial skills, 114, 115
Ergonomic conditions, 94

F

formal mechanisms, 13
Franchising, 16, 137, 138, 139, 144, 145

G

General Management Skills, 118
Gossip Chain, 131, 132
Grapevine, 131, 134

H

Home Employment Directory, 108
home-businesses, 107

I

Individual ownership, 55, 56, 57
Informal communication structures, 131
International Trade Administration, 139

J

Japan, 46

K

Kemetse, Helena, iv

M

Marketing plan, 47
McDonald's, 138
Microsoft Project tools, 48
Mill, John Stewart, 2

N

NatWest/BFA survey, 140

O

Organizational plan, 47

P

Partnership, 55, 56, 57
Patenting Office, 15
Personal Goals, 113
Probability Chain, 132, 133
Production plan, 47
Profit maximization, 143

S

Schumpeter, Joseph, 2, 3, 4

Scientific method, 20, 22
Single Strand Chain, 131, 132
Smith, Adam, 2, 46
style of entrepreneurship, 9

T

TD Industries, 45
Territorial protection, 143
Tucker, Geraldine J., 121, 122, 129, 130, 135, 150

U

United States Chamber of Commerce, 139
University of Krujevac, Serbia, iv

www.ingramcontent.com/pod-product-compliance
Lightning Source LLC
Chambersburg PA
CBHW061744270326
41928CB00011B/2365